Mathodist Episcopal Church

Eighth annual report of the Freedmen's Aid Society of the Methodist Episcopal Church

Mathodist Episcopal Church

Eighth annual report of the Freedmen's Aid Society of the Methodist Episcopal Church

ISBN/EAN: 9783337260101

Printed in Europe, USA, Canada, Australia, Japan

Cover: Foto ©Lupo / pixelio.de

More available books at **www.hansebooks.com**

Eighth Annual Report

OF THE

FREEDMEN'S AID SOCIETY

OF THE

Methodist Episcopal Church.

CINCINNATI:
WESTERN METHODIST BOOK CONCERN PRINT.
1875.

BEQUESTS AND DEVISES

TO THE

FREEDMEN'S AID SOCIETY

OF THE METHODIST EPISCOPAL CHURCH.

PERSONS disposed to make bequests to the Society by Will, are requested to observe the following form:

I give and bequeath to "THE FREEDMEN'S AID SOCIETY OF THE METHODIST EPISCOPAL CHURCH," *a corporation under the laws of the State of Ohio, the sum of* ....; *and the receipt of the Treasurer thereof shall be a sufficient discharge to my Executors for the same.*

FORM OF A DEVISE OF LAND TO SAID BOARD.

I give and devise to "THE FREEDMEN'S AID SOCIETY OF THE METHODIST EPISCOPAL CHURCH," *a corporation under the laws of the State of Ohio, the following land and premises, that is to say:* .... *to have and to hold the same, with the appurtenances, to the said Board, its successors and assigns forever.*

EIGHTH ANNUAL REPORT.

THE Board of Managers of the Freedmen's Aid Society of the Methodist Episcopal Church respectfully submit their Eighth Annual Report:

The past year has been a prosperous one, for which we are profoundly thankful to Almighty God, and the friends of Christian benevolence, who have so generously responded to our appeals for assistance; for in spite of the financial embarrassment of the country, and while there has been a falling off in the collections for almost every other benevolent work, in our own and in other denominations, our receipts for the year have been considerably in advance of those of any preceding one—a fact worthy of especial gratitude, and indicative of the increasing interest of the Church in this important work.

The retrospection of our past efforts in behalf of this injured people awakens mingled emotions of gratitude and sadness: gratitude, that we have been enabled to accomplish so much in an enterprise so intimately connected with the safety of the nation, the elevation of man, and the prosperity of the Church; sadness, that, amid such general desolation, resulting from ignorance, superstition, crime, and slavery, we have been able to contribute so little to the relief and elevation of millions in our midst, suffering the accumulated wrongs of ages.

The work upon which this Society has entered is a gigantic one, and taxes to the utmost the energies and the benevolence of the nation. It is the Christian training of five millions of people, one-eighth of our entire population, and through these the elevation of hundreds of millions of incoming generations. They are now freemen and citizens, endowed with the rights and privileges of citizenship. It must not be forgotten that they were emancipated in ignorance, degradation, and poverty, and are what centuries of wrong and oppression have made them; and it is equally clear that the act of emancipation conferred no preparation for this new condition of life, into which, totally disqualified, they have been thrust. President Lincoln, with a dash of his pen, struck the fetters from the bodies of these four millions of slaves, but their minds were still left in the chains of ignorance, and the iron of slavery had entered into their souls. Emancipation was one of the grandest acts of the nineteenth century, and thrilled with joy the hearts of the people; and forever honored will be the noble men that participated in its achievement; but emancipation is not complete in itself; it presupposes and demands preparation. The nation has emancipated this people; but it has done it at its peril, unless it pushes more vigorously the work of Christian education. We insist upon it that the part we took in emancipation binds us with solemn obligations to educate, for education is the only completion of emancipation; and we are urged to complete this work by every consideration that induced us to commence it. To have emancipated and left these millions in ignorance and degradation would have been a work of doubtful philanthropy, and would have partaken more of the character of crime than of charity. To neglect the preparation of this people would be to perpetuate the wrongs inflicted by slavery, increase the peril of the nation, bring disgrace upon the Church, and provoke the just judgments of heaven. Giving freedom, and preparing its recipients for it, must go hand in hand, else this blood-bought boon is not worth the terrible price it cost.

Justly, the nation regarded the freedmen as its wards, and made provision for their necessities, furnishing food and clothing for their bodies, teachers and books for their minds, thus adding luster to the act of emancipation by securing the necessary qualifications to improve and enjoy it. It can not be too deeply deplored that the clamor against the Freedmen's Bureau was allowed first to cripple, and then to destroy it, before it had accomplished the grand work in which it was engaged; but it lived long enough, in spite of the bitter warfare waged against it, or any mistakes made in its management, to vindicate the wisdom and foresight of its founders, and evidence the paternal regard of the National Government for its wards, as well as to inaugurate a system of schools, that has accomplished more than any other agency in the peaceful settlement of the great questions at issue in the South.

In behalf of the Methodist Episcopal Church, we tender grateful acknowledgments to the Government for the aid received in the erection of school buildings for the education of this emancipated people, regretting that we obtained so small a portion of the Bureau's appropriations, while it was in operation, lamenting the winding up of its affairs, and the cutting off all aid in their behalf. The Freedmen's Bureau, in view of the good accomplished, and its adaptation to the necessities of this people, should have been continued longer. It might have been modified to meet more fully the exigencies of all classes of citizens in the South; any mistakes made in the administration of its affairs might have been corrected, but, in some form or other, the Government should have continued its aid until this unfortunate people had gained strength and intelligence to bear the burdens and discharge the duties imposed upon them by emancipation.

As the Government has retired from this educational work, and as the impoverished condition of the South prevents any large appropriations for education, if this people is educated at all, it must be done by the denominational associations of the North, among which we mention the Freedmen's Aid Society of the Methodist Episcopal Church, which has advanced to the front, in view of the efficient services rendered and the great good accomplished. It is fitting that the Church whose founder took so deep an interest in this race, when it was in bondage, now it is free, and all barriers to its improvement are removed, should put forth vigorous efforts to save it, as it is in accordance with the genius and spirit of this organization to seek among the lost, the poor, the ignorant, and the suffering. The fact that Methodism has so large a constituency among this people, increases its obligations, and assures it of a welcome as broad and enthusiastic as its heroism and benevolence can meet. We must not neglect these helpless members, who appeal so piteously to the "Mother Church" for help, but give to them as God has prospered us.

THE NEGRO PROBLEM.

This is the great problem of the age, and its solution has baffled the skill of our wisest men. Learned divines, profound philosophers, and eminent statesmen have attempted to solve it, but the problem has proved too intricate, and its solution has eluded their grasp. Emancipation has not fully solved it; the negro still comes to the front; and the wisdom of the nation is found inadequate to adjust the rights and harmonize the relations of this freed people with the great majority of the citizens. Ignorance and degradation in the weaker race awaken the prejudice and hostility of the stronger. The conflict rages, and threatens to involve the nation in ruin. Emancipation shivered the fetters from the bodies of this race, but left their minds locked up in ignorance and superstition. In slavery they were guided by the intellect of their masters; in their present degraded condition they are driven by blind impulse and wild passion. They are too ignorant to know what is right; too weak to resist temptation; too self-willed to listen to the appeals of reason; and too depraved to keep God's commandments and live a pure and honest life. To allow this race to remain in the condition emancipation left it, involves the problem in additional difficulties, without removing the peril.

A decade of freedom has made but little progress in its solution. Constitutional amendments, acts of legislation, and political reconstruction in all its phases, have failed in the attainment of the anticipated end. All legislative action that attempts to uplift this people in a mass will prove a failure. It can only be accomplished by individual intelligence and morality. The people must be instructed, and stimulated in regard to personal duties and responsibilities; and character, high-toned Christian character, developed, which will everywhere entitle its possessor to respect and confidence; and these grand results can only be secured by the faithful preaching of the Gospel, and the earnest labor of the Christian teacher. Our national statistics inform us that the freedmen, in spite of predictions, are increasing, and there is no hope of relief from the dying out of the race. There is no prospect of its general removal, either voluntary or involuntary, to some foreign country; for the loss of these laborers would involve the South in bankruptcy and ruin. There is no probability that this people will colonize in any of the Southern States, where there is already a preponderance of the colored element to the exclusion of the white population; for the whites in no State will consent to give up their territory and historic fame to the blacks. There is no probability of such a mingling of these races as shall bleach out the blacks; for freedom has checked the tendency in this direction, so prevalent in slavery. We are forced to this conclusion, that these two races will remain distinct in this country, under the same Government, worshiping the same God, sharing in the common advantages of the nation, and contributing by their lives and property to the common defense.

To prepare the freedmen for this result, the work of education must be inaugurated upon a grander scale, and prosecuted with an energy commensurate with its importance. For only in Christian education do we find the solution of this difficult problem. So soon as the freedmen become intelligent and Christian, they will be respected; prejudice will give way, and cruel treatment disappear. Already they are recognized by the nation as citizens, and invested with its choicest privileges; and the time is not far distant when they will be received and treated with Christian equality by the Church of God. Rome was distinguished for her love of conquest and empire; Greece, for eloquence, poetry, and art; and the proudest boast of America shall be her love of freedom and the rights of man. The great truths of the Fatherhood of God and the brotherhood of man shall yet be fully recognized, and shall exert controlling influence over the heart and life of all men.

URGENCY OF THIS WORK.

The work of Christian education among this people can not be delayed without great peril. The freedmen, at first, were eager to learn; would walk a great distance to attend school, and make great sacrifices for knowledge, for there was a perfect blaze of enthusiasm among them upon this subject. Already a change for the worse is perceptible; for, failing to secure the advantages of the school, the love of books has begun to wane, and the desire for improvement has diminished, and many have fallen into idleness, listlessness, intemperance, and vice. The history of emancipation in the West Indies warns us not to neglect this work; for if we do, the freedmen will become disheartened, and sink down into still deeper degradation; and we shall be compelled to live among an indolent and immoral people, if our free institutions can survive the results of ignorance and crime. A hundred dollars judiciously expended now in educational work, will accomplish five times as much as at some subsequent time. In view of the urgent demands of this work, the peril of the nation and the Church, and the fearful effects of delay upon the freedmen, the Managers have allowed the Secretary, in two or three extreme cases, to anticipate its income, and make investments for school property, in order that we might inaugurate our work and prepare, as speedily as possible, preachers and teachers to meet the demands of our mission in the South. But this is a deviation from the settled policy of our Society, and can not without danger be repeated in the future.

Those intending to make, or having made, bequests to this cause, would greatly increase the value of their benefactions by making them available now, when so much more good might be accomplished by these funds, rather than by waiting till near the close of life to make a donation or bequest; for the donor would have the assurance that his gift had been appropriated to the object for which it had been donated, and the fruits of it might cheer his heart prior to his departure from earth to heaven. This is the golden moment for the salvation of this people, and if neglected, the most disastrous consequences may follow. The best part of time enough yet, for the accomplishment of any great good, is the first part; and for the freedmen this is rapidly passing away; and it is as clear as sunlight that there will never be another so favorable an opportunity for rendering valuable assistance to this unfortunate race. It is possible now, as in childhood, to pre-empt it for Christ; but to allow this people to drift still farther away into superstition, infidelity, and vice, when they might now be saved by Christian education, and thus render the chances of their salvation extremely difficult, if not hopeless, seems to be a policy too short-sighted and suicidal to be allowed by American Christians.

The great duty of the hour, the one that should be impressed upon the mind and conscience of the Church and nation as pre-eminent at this crisis, is the salvation of these five millions of colored people in our midst, who, in the providence of God, seem designed to play so important a part in the destinies of this nation. This race is looked upon as a prize to be secured, for personal, political, or ecclesiastical aggrandizement. Rome is planning upon a gigantic scale to proselyte and make it subservient to its wily schemes; and Romanists are prodigal in their expenditures for this purpose; political demagogues are striving to secure their votes to ride into power and office, while they sacrifice every interest vital to the welfare of the freedmen to their own personal emolument; and parties, and sects, and different sections of the country, regard these poor people as legitimate spoils. Truly, their condition is a sad one, and the outlook fearful. Unless help, on a scale commensurate to the magnitude of the interest in peril, speedily come, consequences too appalling for contemplation will overtake us. While we hesitate in the vigorous prosecution of this work, the race drifts away from our influence, the Church suffers, and the republic trembles in the balances. No more urgent work for Christ and fallen humanity challenges our attention anywhere upon the face of this round world. No other people of equal population can be neglected by us at a hazard so disastrous. No greater obligations urge us to engage in any other mission of usefulness, nor do any other fields of culture promise earlier or more bountiful harvests.

PIETY OF THE FREEDMEN.

As we have more than one hundred and fifty thousand colored members in our Church in the South, and as very severe criticism has been indulged in regard to the piety of the freedmen, we ask attention to the following impartial reflections: This is a topic of grave import, and demands great candor in its discussion. We must avoid the extremes of opinion submitted on this subject; and while we admit that the type of piety among the freedmen is extremely defective, we claim that it is genuine, possessing an experience of pardoned sin, consciousness of acceptance with God, and the realization of the consolations of the Holy Ghost. That the light of their Christian experience and faith should be dimmed by the darkness of slavery is to be expected; it would be very strange if it were otherwise. Trained for centuries in the school of oppression, where almost every distinction between right and wrong has been frittered away, it would be surprising if the freedmen were models of morality or Christian consistency.

Their piety must, in the very nature of the case, be affected by their ignorance and degradation. The religion of Christ demands purity of thought and act,—difficult attainments for those dwarfed by ignorance and demoralized by slavery; and it would be unreasonable to expect the highest specimens of Christian integrity from the lowest grade of humanity; for as in water face answereth to face, so among this people does piety in active life to knowledge; and babes in intelligence as they are can only be expected to be babes in morality; and those who have advanced no farther in their education than the alphabet should not be required to unravel the mysteries of the science of salvation, or furnish the brightest illustrations of Christian integrity. The type of the ex-slave's piety corresponds to the knowledge of his obligations to God and his fellow-men; and any improvement of it must be secured by an increase of knowledge, obtained from God's Word, pertaining to the duties of life, accompanied by the influence of the Holy Spirit. It is the personal perusal of the inspired Word, accompanied by earnest prayer for heavenly illumination and strength, that secures aid from above to lift the soul up into a higher plane, produce the renovation of the nature, and fortify against the temptations of life.

When the Bible was prohibited from the slaves by fearful penalties, then we have reason to believe that Jehovah deigned to hold communion with this unfortunate people by his blessed Spirit; He enlightened their minds, guided their lives, and comforted their souls in their night of suffering and sorrow. But the times of that ignorance over which the slaves had no control, God winked at, but now commandeth all men every-where to repent of sin, read his Word, and believe on his Son. Slavery has been overthrown; intelligence must supplement emancipation, and the freedmen must learn from God's Word, what in the weakness of their minds and the darkness of the times was communicated to them by the Holy Spirit.

Instruction from illiterate ministers, who can scarcely read the Bible themselves, may do something for this people, but it can not secure the highest type of Christian character. It must not, however, be inferred that they are not Christians, even though they be defective in character and inconsistent in life, boisterous and fanatical in worship. Their whole nature is demoralized by slavery, and though ignorance and superstition, and even questionable morality, may cloud and mar their piety, yet, amid it all, there is deep penitence, strong faith, and unshaken confidence in God. Education and experience and faithful preaching will gradually drive away fanaticism and superstition, and introduce a pure morality and a simple worship. What is good and true in the Churches must be retained and strengthened, and what is false and fanatical removed, and the character of the membership modeled upon the New Testament standard. The school-house and the meeting-house, with intelligent and Christ-like teachers, will, with the blessing of God, bring about this glorious result.

We must recognize, in our treatment of this question, touching the genuineness of the piety of the freedmen, that emotion as well as thought is essential to piety, that religious development is scarcely less dependent upon feeling than thinking, and that thought only ripens into golden fruit when quickened by the inspiration of emotion. Even truth itself in the intellect lies cold and dormant, till it enters into the affections, inflames the soul, and quickens its possessor to a sublime faith and a heroic life. The poor, ignorant freedmen, worshiping God with all the light they have, struggling to perform the stern duties of life with a trustful heart, as well as the scholar and philosopher, are precious in God's sight, and shall share in the joys of his kingdom.

An emotional religion, then, must not be indiscriminately condemned; for it is the only religion that can meet the wants of a large class of this fallen world. We must take care, in educating the freedmen, that we do not substitute cold formality, and an intellectual appreciation of the truth, for an enthusiastic religious experience and a warm heart. Many of the freedmen are, without doubt, Christians, and though they may indulge in a mode of life and worship displeasing to intelligent Christians, and in striking contrast with the strict requirements of God's law; yet great allowances should be made, in view of their history, ignorance and degradation; for, in spite of their inconsistencies of life, they exhibit a faith in God, and confidence in his protection and love, that wins our respect, and entitles them to recognition as the followers of Christ. We offer no apology for, but enter the strongest condemnation of, the lack of high-toned morality in these professors of religion; but we protest against excluding them from our Christian love and the household of faith, while we implore for them a pure Gospel and ministry, and facilities for obtaining Christian education, whereby they may attain unto a higher and purer life, become examples of robust Christian character, and successful laborers in the vineyard of the Lord.

ROMANISM.

It is not safe to disguise the fact that Romanists are directing especial attention to the freedmen, and in the absence of suitable efforts on the part of Protestants they may yet be successful. Not until they had votes to cast did they take any interest in their welfare. The Papists of the Old World, under the auspices of the Pope of Rome and Archbishop Manning, are sending missionaries in rapid succession to labor among this people. They are in dead earnest in this matter, and have sagacity enough to see that their only chance for supremacy in this country is to proselyte the freedmen. They have vast resources at their disposal, and expend them freely in the accomplishment of their schemes. The freedmen are so anxious to learn that they will attend poor schools taught by the Papists, unless Protestants furnish good ones. But the teachings of Romanists disqualify the freedmen from becoming loyal citizens or intelligent Christians. This Papal movement should be an incentive to renewed effort and zeal from all Protestants, who should every-where unite in the common cause of educating this people, and thus save them from the wiles of Romanism; for whoever aids and educates them in their ignorance and suffering will have their hearty co-operation in the future. If Protestants educate this race, they anchor it to Protestantism; if Romanists do it, then

Romanism controls it. As in our past struggles, so in this, self-interest, to say nothing of the higher motives of patriotism, philanthropy and Christianity, urges us to the work of educating this race, as the only way in which our free institutions may be preserved. The colored people may be saved to Protestantism; and with their co-operation and the blessing of God, this nation may withstand the assaults of Romanism and the attacks of any other foe, at home or abroad.

What is demanded at the present crisis is an awakening of the people to the peril that threatens us. Our danger is in apathy, not in our inability to resist and conquer this foe. Normal and Biblical schools must be sustained and endowed, and the youth welcomed to these privileges; missionaries must be multiplied, meeting-houses erected, Bibles scattered, intelligence disseminated, and the people instructed. There is no agency so well adapted to confront this foe as the Freedmen's Aid Society. It is in the field with enlarged experience; its schools are judiciously located, in central places; its teachers are efficient, enthusiastic, and pious; and only the means are wanted. Give it the money demanded for its work, and, in connection with other Protestant societies, it will save the South from the triumph of Romanism. Methodism, with the spirituality of its worship, increases its antagonistic power against Romanism, and meets a great want of the negro, whose heart is peculiarly susceptible to religious impressions. Class and prayer and camp meetings, fervent preaching and exhortation, the singing of spiritual hymns, and the relating of Christian experience, are more than a match for all the ceremony and display of the Romish Church. Methodism, with the funds, and the honest recognition of Christian brotherhood, may defeat Rome, and save the nation.

It becomes us to study carefully the providence of God in the emancipation of this race, and in placing it within our reach as a grand reserve, in the terrible conflict that has already begun to wage, in this country, between ignorance and intelligence, the Papal and the free schools—Romanism and Protestantism. The importance of our educational work, in the light of this thought, can not be overestimated. It appeals to us in tones that should startle us from slumber, and urge to more vigorous action. To neglect it is to peril interests vital to Christian civilization. It is to fling away one of the grandest opportunities ever presented to save a race, and bind it with indissoluble bonds to Christ and the Republic.

INSTITUTIONS.

The Society has aided in the establishment and support of the following institutions:

> Central Tennessee College, Nashville, Tenn.
> Shaw University, Holly Springs, Miss.
> Claflin University and Baker Institute, Orangeburg, S. C.
> Clark University and Theological Seminary, Atlanta, Ga.
> New Orleans University and Thomson Biblical Institute, New Orleans.
> Wiley University, Marshall, Texas.
> Haven Normal School, Waynesboro, Ga.
> Rust Biblical and Normal Institute, Huntsville, Ala.
> La Teche Seminary, Baldwin, La.
> Bennett Seminary, Greensboro, N. C.
> Richmond Normal School, Richmond, Va.
> Cookman Institute, Jacksonville, Florida.
> Centenary Biblical Institute, Baltimore, Md.
> Orphans' Home, Baldwin, La.

In addition to the above institutions of a higher grade, the Society has aided in the support of many common-schools.

The influence of this Society is felt all over the South. Fifty thousand have been taught in its day and a larger number in its Sunday schools. Hundreds of preachers now laboring among this people, and thousands of teachers instructing the children, have been taught in institutions established and sustained by this Society, which has provided in the South a school property worth more than two hundred thousand dollars. It is estimated that more than forty thousand children, have been taught by those trained in our schools, so successfully does this work perpetuate itself. A society that has done so grand a work as this, bears the seal of divine approbation, and deserves liberal support from the Church and the Government. Our mission work in the South could not have been planted, and can not be sustained, without our schools; and we must liberally sustain this educational work among the poor freedmen of the South, or prove recreant to the highest obligations of humanity, and incur the displeasure of God.

CENTRAL TENNESSEE COLLEGE.

Rev. J. Braden, D. D., President.
Rev. J. W. Patterson, A. M., Professor of Languages.
Rev. Otis Cole, Professor of Theology.
Rev. J. H. Whitney, Professor of Natural Science.
Miss Ella V. Plotner, Professor of Mathematics.
Mrs. Otis Cole, Professor of Music.

This institution is situated on Maple Street, Nashville, Tennessee. The buildings are four—composed of brick. The residence is a plain substantial building, two stories high, and contains fourteen rooms, used for teachers, music rooms and students. The second building is also two stories high, and contains a chapel thirty-six by sixty feet on the first floor, and twelve rooms in the second story, used for dormitories. The third building is what has heretofore been used as a school building, *three* stories *high*, containing twenty-eight rooms, now occupied as the boarding-hall. The dining-room, kitchen, store-room and laundry occupy the first floor, the teachers, their families and lady students the remaining rooms. The last is a four story building, a commanding, plain and substantial structure, fifty-two by ninety feet, with a capacious basement. The two lower stories contain school and recitation rooms, library, cabinet, reading and society rooms. The two upper stories are divided into dormitories for students. This building contains forty-eight rooms, besides four large ones in the basement. The value of this entire property is more than $70,000. It is capable of accommodating in all departments three hundred students.

This school was commenced in 1866 in one of our churches in Nashville. Later it was moved into "The Gun Factory," which had been originally intended as a manufactory of guns for the Confederate army, but by the vicissitudes of war, it was used as a hospital by the Federals, and then for three years as a school for Freedmen. The present site for the school was purchased in 1868, and the school opened in the parlors of the family residence, which could only accommodate fifty students. In 1869 the Freedmen's Bureau erected the present boarding-hall and the chapel, and made repairs on the residence, amounting to twenty thousand dollars. The Church, through the Missionary and Freedmen's Aid Societies, has furnished the rest that has been spent in the buildings, excepting what the Tennesseeans have saved by their charming concerts. The teachers have been supported by our Freedmen's Aid Society. The attendance of students has averaged over two hundred annually. Last year the catalogue showed two hundred and forty. A large proportion of the students are preparing to teach school or preach the Gospel. Hundreds have already gone out from the college, and are now successfully engaged in teaching. Those who have attended the Theological department have been useful to the Church, and now occupy some of the most responsible positions in the conferences. The number of these students in attendance is comparatively small, for the want of means to meet their expenses. Many already in the conferences would be at the college could they find some benevolent person to aid them. A few will, with the consent of the conference, leave their work, if only for two or three months, attend school, and get such instruction as will aid them in the ministry. With a little aid for each, scores of promising young men might be gathered into this department, who would prove a blessing to the Church, and to their people, as heralds of the cross.

The advancement of the students has been all that could reasonably be expected. We have a small class of Freshmen. The students who were as far advanced as the Freshman class four years ago, have been teaching and preaching, and so great has been the demand for their services, and their poverty, that they have not returned to finish their course. Only the younger students we are able to retain till they have completed their course of study in the literary department. In the theological school young men will stay as long as their conscience, the voice of the Church, and their money will permit. The demand is so great, that teachers and preachers are taken from the school with very limited qualifications; yet such are the necessities of the colored people, that this is the best that can be done. The future of this educational work is full of promise. They are feeling more and more the necessity of higher qualification for the school-room and the pulpit, as well as for professional life. They have, themselves, now a much higher estimate of the value of education than when they first came out of bondage.

There is an increasing demand for the higher qualification of the teacher and preacher. This our schools, supported by the Freedmen's aid Society, are endeavoring to meet. The intimate relation that the educational work among the Freedmen sustains to our whole work in the South is evident to any one who has examined the results of the work of the Methodist Episcopal Church in the South. An interest in education has been aroused in all our conferences, and a determination to have better facilities for education is manifesting itself in the erection of seminaries and academies. These schools for whites are important to the success and permanency of our work in that direction, and deserve the fostering care of the Church.

The Freedmen's schools, established at centers of influence, have tended very largely to impress this fact upon the people, that, the Methodist Episcopal Church does not consent to be perpetually shut out from any part of the parish that the founder of Methodism claimed for himself and his followers. And these school buildings have exerted a wonderful influence upon the colored people. To them, they have been the assurances of interest in their welfare of most substantial worth. Whatever efforts may have been made to prejudice the colored people against our Church, this work of the Freedmen's Aid Society has answered the enemy, fully and finally. Then, the work of the students of these schools, has been such as to commend itself and the schools to the Church and the colored people. Not only do the teachers instruct their pupils during the week, but they are leaders in organizing and keeping up Sunday-schools in connection with the day schools.

If this work is followed up and sustained by the Church, as the circumstances demand, the future of the people of the South will be wonderfully benefited. The financial prosperity of the Southern States depends upon the morality and intelligence of the people; and the work already performed by the Freedmen's Aid Society is telling with wonderful results on the interests of the colored people. They have learned something of economy, of the value of money, the duties of husband and wife, the relation of labor to independence, and the duties to the country and to God which their freedom enjoins upon them. The necessity for the work of the Society still remains.

Never was there a more inviting field for Christian labor or Christian benevolence. The Freedmen are to be what the Church makes them—under the Divine blessing, a source of strength to Protestantism, to morality, to intelligence and financial prosperity; or neglected, they will become the tools of unprincipled demagogues, a source of corruption to morals, and financially an expense to the nation. Which it will be does not entirely depend on our Church, but there is no branch of the Church of God that shares more largely in the responsibility for the future of the colored people of the South, than does the Methodist Episcopal Church. Whether we meet our responsibilities, or not, depends upon the ten thousand pastors, who, if they will but present this claim, will answer the question, to the glory of God, and the highest good of a people who, from their past history, have peculiar claims upon the sympathies and charities of the entire Church.

A FIELD-DAY AT NASHVILLE.

BY BISHOP HAVEN.

NOWHERE in the South has our educational work put on a better shape than at Central Tennessee College. The southern building is the original mansion purchased with the surrounding land. It is a spacious brick building containing, this conference week, some twenty visitors. Next above it is Thomson Chapel, a neat brick two-story building, as goodly a chapel as can be found in half the colleges of the country, and better than can be found in the other half. Middletown, till Dr. Cummings resigned, had nothing half as good, nor Wilbraham before Dr. Raymond's day; Indiana Asbury has not yet, and the Ohio Wesleyan has nothing to surpass it.

Next to the chapel is the recitation building, now changed into boarding rooms. Each of these buildings has dormitories over it, the first, one story additional to the chapel, and the second, two. Each is a neat brick structure, plain to simplicity, as are all the old college buildings of America and Europe; each a little taller than its predecessor. Then comes, a hundred feet off, the new building, which is yet unnamed, but which protemporally, we shall call Rust Hall, for to no one is it so greatly indebted for its existence as to him. It rises four stories high, each story ten to twelve feet, with basement and attics, giving it a lofty elevation of nearly fifty feet. It is ninety feet long and fifty-two feet wide, built of brick, with grayish brown blinds to its long windows, the whole capped with a neat turret and belfry. It is a better academic building than many of your Northern colleges yet enjoy. It properly crowns and completes the campus.

At two o'clock we enter the chapel to attend the dedicatory exercises. It is crowded with as happy and as handsome an audience as ever Methodism saw together in the North or South. The services were under the direction of Dr. Braden. Rev. Mr. Hayes, an alumnus of the college, read the first hymn, and how it was sung you ought to have been there to have heard. Well, if caste is in song, these are the Brahmins and all the rest of us Pariahs. Rev. Mr. Pickett, Presiding Elder, like Brother Hayes, once a slave, led in prayer. Rev. Mr. Mason, son of the Book Agent of my youth, and also presiding elder, read the Scriptures. Again the school blossomed into song, and the address followed of the President of the Board of Trustees to the presiding Bishop, presenting the edifice to him for dedication. It was brief, and referred to the great changes that were revived by these scenes. Like a prairie in June, one was bewildered with flowers. Whichever way the thought turned it was saluted by rich results. The Virgilian wanderers in the midst of their distresses comforted themselves with the thought that afterward it would be delightful to remember these griefs; so we, from this height of bliss, could look back to the darkness and danger of earlier days. Nine years ago he saw this school in linsey-woolsey gowns, and ragged jackets and trousers, without shoes, without knowledge, without culture, almost without a consciousness of humanity. How changed! So handsomely appareled, so comely of countenance, so intelligent, so self-reliant. They were urged to grow in these graces, and be worthy of the vocation wherewith they were called. In closing he referred to the fact that they were not out of peril yet. A year ago he saw the pleasant face of Julia Hayden; but she had been shot dead in her bed because she dared to be a teacher. Dangers still stood thick through all the ground; but God was over us, protecting and guiding, and would yet bring all our enemies to respect and to love us. Nashville was losing its mercantile and political headship, but was gaining the supremacy in letters. Five or six educational institutions of high grade had been established here—four of them since the war. He rejoiced over the existence of all these colleges girdling the city, and trusted they would work harmoniously and happily for the common elevation and Christianization of the whole State, region, and country.

Bishop Bowman followed in a beautiful address on the benefits of education. He contrasted those humble beginnings which he himself had witnessed with these grand conclusions. He had never felt so proud on any day of his life, except on a few such notable personal epochs. He showed how needed education was for the uplifting of labor and the reduction of crime. Of one-third more value was educated than uneducated labor, and three-fourths of the crime was committed by uneducated persons. He demanded the maintenance of the common-school against atheism and Romanism, and also declared that all higher education should and must be Christian. He plead glowingly for the culture of these people, who had so long sat in enforced darkness, and depicted the results of such colleges as this. It was an admirable address, stimulant and progressive.

Dr. Rust enjoyed himself, and the audience enjoyed him also, as he waved his sword of victory over this field, under the old Methodist flag. And he well might glory. All of this he had seen, and the most of it he had been. He spoke of the degradation in which he found these pupils, and what had crushed them so. Slavery had driven its plow-share beam deep through every mental and moral human faculty; slavery had crushed out manhood, and then had declared they were incapable of manhood. The Church that by its inspiration and its soldiery had liberated their bodies, was now engaged in the grander work of emancipating their minds and souls. He, exulting, pointed to these proofs before us of its zeal and of its success. His remarks were vociferously received.

Professor Spence, of Fisk University, said that he was taught by his mother the horribleness of slavery—that in this land of ours they sold little children from their mothers and parents from each other; that when he came to Nashville after the war, and first saw the flag flying from the State House, he rejoiced that this flag no longer meant union and slavery, but union and liberty. He congratulated the college on its prosperity.

Rev. Mr. Phillips, the able President of the Baptist College, made a quaint and attractive address. He said the descendants of Ham were the earliest civilizers. From them we received letters and arts and arms. If every descendant of Ham was to be reckoned of negro origin, then David was a mulatto, and in the veins of Christ ran negro blood. As no Caucasian or Japhetic blood can be traced to Christ, it gives the Hamite unquestioned pre-eminence. He thought the time would come when they would again impart the learning they had once bestowed.

Professor Bennett, of Fisk University, said the Methodists had shown great common sense in their buildings here. Each was higher than its former neighbor, so that, if a line were stretched from the roof of the first to the last, it would touch each roof between in due order on its upward scale. If they went on in this way they might yet reach heaven by successive steps upward of their ascending buildings. He was surprised that no Church in the South had ever concerned itself with the education of these four millions of its people.

Judge Caldwell gave a stirring speech, telling how, once a slaveholder, he became an abolitionist. He saw a child of two years sold from its mother. She stood weeping by. So did its father. As he went home and saw his tottling two-year-old come out to meet him, and took it in his arms he vowed eternal hate to a system so cruel. He said he gloried in being a member of the Northern Yankee Nigger Methodist Church. When his rebel enemies taunt him with being "a nigger worshiper," he retorts, "How many mulatto children have you?" The reply is always a dead shot. The Judge is reserve delegate to the General Conference.

Following him came Rev. Calvin Pickett, who described his previous condition of servitude, and his gladness at liberation. He was full of humorous hits, and concluded by saying: "When the fetters and withes and cords and grape-vines that bound me fell from me, I weighed a hundred and sixty pounds; now I weigh two hundred and sixteen." That was a new argument in proof of the beneficial effects of liberty, and a "clincher.'

Dr. Braden concluded the addresses by some feeling words. He declared education would not cure this prejudice of caste. It was only by getting low at the foot of the Cross. There the chains of this bondage would fall from us, and we would feel the blessed oneness of all in Christ Jesus.

The audience, held for three hours in ceaseless pleasure and profit, sang the doxology, and were dismissed by Bishop Bowman. They poured over the new building, which was pronounced eminently satisfactory. It cost only $20,000, and is a marvel of cheapness. Its recitation-rooms are large and high; its dormitories better than three-fourths, if not nine-tenths, of the colleges afford. They need to be comfortably furnished. What Sunday-schools will send Dr. Rust fifty dollars each for furnishing a room in this college? Our Church must help pay these bills. We shall soon have a law department added to the others. The teachers are able and popular, and the college is destined to be a power in the State. The kingdom of God cometh not with observation. The grand gift of a Northern millionaire, who arose from the lowest station in society because society did not forbid his rise, and did not insult, degrade, oppress, and enslave him, has taken goodly shape. It came with observation. It has been accompanied with observation in all its stately steps. Governor and judges and soldiery and ecclesiastics and a thronging multitude attended its opening. Here an unknown and despised few in a rude factory commenced together an unknown and more despised class; and little by little it has grown to these proportions. Nearly seventy-five thousand dollars have gone into this enterprise, and though to-day local journals may speak timidly or contemptuously of it, still they, and all, near and far, are beginning to see that this, which came without observation, is, indeed, the kingdom of God that is being set up in this place and form, with rejoicings on earth and rejoicings in heaven. Her haughty sister, changed in heart, shall yet see and hail her as her own kindred in the Lord, and she shall find in her former enemy her loving and lasting companion. This great day in our Southern Zion has more than a local significance. When some wisely foolish brethren are urging that to bring about another union, we should, as one of our colored brethren in New Orleans said, "put us niggers out," the Church, by her buildings and benefactions, is so interweaving herself with "us niggers" that she will have to put herself out if she puts out them. So far will this sin and crime be from her door that she will the more closely knit herself to these her brethren, affection for whom, service to whom, identification with whom, is the only test of her real Churchhood to-day.

Not sanctification raptures in Northern camp-grounds and Churches, but devotion to these Christ's children, in captivity and contumely, is to be the real test in that day of the Christ-like condition of the believer. We shall be knit closer to these our brothers, and feel that they are beloved in the flesh and in the Lord, until all this cloud of shame and sin vanish away, and these halls be filled with students of every hue, studying, and worshiping in loving unity. That platform, that audience, the spirit of that hour, assure that consummation. Come, Lord Jesus, and come quickly!

SHAW UNIVERSITY.

Rev. A. C. M'Donald, D. D., President.
Rev. W. W. Hooper, A. M., Principal.
C. A. Weaver, A. M., Professor of Mathematics.
Mrs. M. A. Weaver, Teacher.
Mrs. W. W. Hooper, Teacher.

The past twelve months with us have been full of earnest wearisome toil, and fraught with varied experiences: at one time giving bright hopes of speedy success, at another, bringing discouragements thick and fast, till we have been almost ready to sink down weary and sad, exclaiming: "They have been so long in darkness, they can not be raised!" But recounting the wonderful works of Him, who in ages past taught his people and raised them from the grossest idolatry and superstition to a faithful worship of the true God, we arose, doubled our efforts and pushed forward in the good work with renewed strength and hopes. And now, at the close of the year, in reviewing the past, we have great reason to thank God and take courage. We have enrolled during the year upward of two hundred students, who have averaged an attendance of six months each. More than one hundred of this number have taught at least three months during the year, having an average attendance of above fifty pupils each, making more than *five thousand pupils* that have been directly or indirectly under the influence of our University during the year. The great majority of these have not only received mental but spiritual instruction. And who shall estimate the vastness of the harvest that the future will reap from the seed thus sown?

Our institution is located in a State having a colored population of 444,201 to 382,896 of whites, and from the natural characteristics of the State, it must for generations to come, have a very large colored element. This element is now largely under the influence of our Church, and if the proper educational efforts are put forth it may be brought much more fully under our control. Our principal competitors for such controlling influence, is not the Baptist Church, though about equal to us numerically, nor the Cobgregational Church, surpassing us in educational efforts, but the much more shrewd and far-seeing Roman Catholic. Even in Holly Springs, under the shadow of our University, they are using those arts of which they are such skillful masters, so well calculated to decoy their unsuspecting victims. Special services are held and special efforts are being made, and these are not without success. As here, so all over the State, they are carrying forward their deep laid schemes and insinuating themselves into the confidence of this people, so susceptible and so easily influenced by ceremony and parade. Success in their movements would be religiously and politically deplorable. This is to be a fearful struggle, the more fearful because we know not at what moment the enemy will have us by the throat, so stealthy are his movements; and unless we are awake and vigorous in our efforts, we shall be trampled in the dust. There is no weapon stronger and more dreaded by this foe than that of free education.

For this and other reasons, it becomes our duty to make ample provisions for the thorough instruction of the youths in all that tends to elevate and enlighten.

It is our aim to do no hot-house work, seeking to hurry students through a college curriculum, as do many mushroom schools in the South, sending them into the battle of life only to disgrace themselves and bring reproach upon the cause of education at large, but take the by far more difficult and tedious plan of trying to lay well a foundation for a broad, thorough, and practical education, such as shall fit our pupils for long lives of usefulness to themselves, their race, and the Church. To do this takes time, tools, shops, and brains variously exercised and severely taxed. All these cost money, and when we compare what we are receiving for this purpose, with what is given to Northern schools, we really wonder that we have done so much. Our students and friends here are increasing their aid each year, many parents really suffering for food and clothing that they may keep their children in school, the school of their accepted Church; and some students walking three and five miles to school each day. Our location as a town is both beautiful and healthful, and our college site is surpassed by few in any State. However hostile to the education of the Freedmen the whites may be elsewhere, in the South, here both teachers and pupils are respected and encouraged by the most influential of them. One of the first men of this place, an ex-slave-holder, has voluntarily taken it upon himself to raise means for us among his people. We are greatly in need of a new building, and increased facilities for educational purposes, and unless we can secure an additional school edifice adapted to our necessities, our work must greatly suffer. Who will help us?

We could bring to our University the most promising young men in the State, and prepare them for extensive usefulness in our schools and pulpits, if we only had our college edifice completed.

CLAFLIN UNIVERSITY.

BY REV. EDWARD COOKE, D. D., PRESIDENT.

This institution is located in the borough of Orangeburg, S. C., on the railroad from Charleston to Columbia, the capital of the State. Prior to the late war it was a Presbyterian school of first-class reputation, known as the Orangeburg Female College. After the war the property was purchased, through the personal efforts of Dr. A. Webster and Rev. T. W. Lewis, and opened as a school for colored youth of both sexes. A charter of ample powers was conferred by the State, under the name of Claflin University, in honor of the late Honorable Lee Claflin, of Massachusetts, by whose liberality, together with that of his distinguished son, ex-Governor Claflin, in connection with the Freedmen's Aid Society, the institution is chiefly indebted for what it has been and what it now is.

The property is a valuable one; a creditable beginning of what is destined in the future, if properly cared for by the Church, to become a great moral power for the elevation of the colored race. It is already beginning to exhibit fruit like Wilbraham, Cazenovia, and other of our older seminaries at the North. It is preparing young men of promise for the ministry in the Methodist Episcopal Church; is sending out large numbers of both sexes to become teachers in the public-schools of the State; and, under its training, others are preparing for professional, scientific, mechanical, and agricultural life. But with all this great work on its hands, it has no endowments to support its teachers, nor are its pupils able to pay any tuition. It must be sustained and the teachers paid by the voluntary contributions of friends to the enterprise. The colored people are not yet able to do it; it must be done, if at all, chiefly at the North. That elect lady, the widow of the noble man whose name it bears, and other members of the family, are contributing liberally for its support, but they can not be expected to do all that is required. The whole Church has a responsibility in this work.

Competent and self-sacrificing teachers are laboring faithfully for God and his Church in this mission field. Brethren, shall they be sustained? Shall they receive the pittance promised as necessary to keep them in the work, or shall they be compelled to abandon it and return North, because the Church does not respond to the claim?

Almost every week good and promising young men, burning with zeal for God, write us and inquire: "Can you help us to get an education, that we may be the better prepared to preach Christ to the people?" The same question is, I suppose, asked all over the South. Brethren, it is for you to say how we shall answer these pressing applications. How many such, thirsting for knowledge, would have their hearts gladdened and purposes strengthened by the aid of fifty or even twenty-five dollars a year!

No mission field in the wide world presents stronger claims, nor makes surer returns for what is bestowed, than the work among the colored population of the South. But they must have help. The time will come when they will be able to endow their own schools, build their own churches, and support their own preachers; but they can not do it now.

The future history of our common country—the rich legacy bequeathed by our fathers—hangs with breathless interest upon the solution of this Southern question. Brethren of the North, shall this work be sustained?

CLARK UNIVERSITY,
ATLANTA, GEORGIA.

BY REV. ISAAC J. LANSING, A. M., PRESIDENT.

We came to this work October 1, 1874. It had been carried on previously by those devoted servants of God, Rev. J. W. Lee and wife, of the Georgia Conference. At that time, the only accommodations for the school, including the boarding and recitation rooms, consisted of a substantial house of eleven rooms. In addition to this, a plain wooden building was erected in October, twenty-six by forty-six feet, two stories high, the lower story divided by folding-doors into two recitation-rooms, the upper forming dormitories for boys, costing twelve hundred dollars. The American Stove Works, of New York City, through the friendly influence of one of the officers of the Company, Mr. Sanford, of the Methodist Episcopal Church, gave us a furnace of capacity to heat the school-rooms.

Though the year has been remarkable for deep poverty and distress among the colored people, our school has had an aggregate attendance of one hundred and twenty-two students, thirty-two of them boarders. On account of their poverty, many of these have spent only a short time with us; but some have been able to remain throughout the school year. These have improved manifestly. The aggregate receipts from students for board and tuition have amounted to about one thousand dollars. Several donations from kind friends have been received and applied to the support of poor and deserving students, and the Board of Education of the Methodist Episcopal Church has given valuable aid to the amount of three hundred dollars.

Classes have been instructed in common English, in elocution, physical geography, physiology, book-keeping, algebra, Latin, Greek, and Bible history. A series of discourses, adapted to the understanding of all the scholars, has been given on the "Young Men and Women of the Bible," and the lessons of their lives, considered in historical order. For the especial benefit of those who intend to be teachers, a course of normal lectures has been delivered in the hearing of the entire school. During the Winter, also, a course of lectures and readings was arranged for the entertainment and instruction of the scholars and their friends. These were well attended and much appreciated.

At the beginning of the year a Sunday-school was opened, and preaching services were regularly held, the Sunday-school having an average attendance of a hundred scholars. A donation of books from the London Religious Tract Society, sent by Rev. Dr. Hatfield, furnished some literature for our Sunday-school, and also duplicate copies sufficient to give a suitable book to each member of the day-school on the occasion of our Christmas celebration. The Sunday-school holds its session at three o'clock on Sabbath afternoons, and every Sabbath morning our students act as teachers and superintendents of other Sunday-schools of our Churches in the city. All these schools are growing encouragingly, three of them having been organized within the year, so that already more than three hundred scholars are gathered into them, and the number is increasing. This work has been greatly assisted by the use of the singing-book known as "Song Life," by Philip Phillips, one hundred and seventy-six copies of which were generously donated us by the author. Though the native songs of the captivity, when sung by the Tennesseeans, charm our cultivated Northern audiences by their novelty and pathos, still their uncouth language and meaningless repetitions have an unfavorable effect upon our rising people here. Refining music, with words full of elevated sentiment, supplement our instructions instead of overturning them, as do many of the plantation songs. Our brother's gift was, therefore, most opportune, and sweet songs ringing through our buildings, elevating the thoughts, impressing the heart, and purifying the life, form a wonderful contrast to the "college music" of many more favored schools among more favored youth.

This outline of our work would be far from complete unless it embraced a brief statement of the *principles* on which it is carried out, its apparent *effects*, and an indication of *our needs* for its futherance. I am oppressed by thoughts which demand utterance, for which this report does not furnish space.

As the social position of the colored people, present and future, is most discussed, you will be interested to know that we "perceive that God is no respecter of persons." This truth of God we seek to learn and to teach by precept and example. We insist that the true difference between men, determining their position in the sight of God, is in character, not color; and we enforce this truth by treating our students as we would wish to be treated under like circumstances. We sit in the same dining-room and eat at the same table, conversing with them as we would with any persons of similar age and attainments. As to their future social position, we urge them to be worthy of any society and to intrude into none.

Without prejudging their mental capacity, we incite them to study all branches of truth, from the lowest upward, and we spend no time in endeavoring to prove their mental equality with any body, excepting what we spend in teaching them. All our instruction purposes to show them God. Our first and prevailing desire is that they may attain such a character, by the grace of God, as will make it certain that what they learn will be well used. Daily, in every branch of study, we teach and preach Christ. With this purpose we teach heartily and hopefully whatever relates to the present conduct of life, all practical knowledge now especially needful to them, and in addition all the higher branches designed to more perfectly discipline their powers. While the results of our work are trusted to God, he kindly vouchsafes to us some very encouraging views of apparent benefits.

All boarding in the house seem to have become soundly converted to God. They give the best evidence of piety which we can have in their humble profession of faith and godly living. Their real Christianity is not wanting in any of the marks by which we have been accustomed to judge of the soundness of the experience of young people in other places. In these six months past we have not heard a vile or profane word from any of our young men. They are strictly temperate, abstaining wholly from liquors and tobacco, are truthful likewise, and virtuous in conduct. Neatness and taste characterize their dress. Carelessness is the exception, and that it is so is all the more to their credit, when you remember that many of them dwell at home in miserable cabins of only one room, and their clothing is often of the poorest fabric. To this testimony as to their care of their persons I must add a strong commendation of their general good manners and courtesy. At table, in the school-room, on the street, in church, and wherever I have seen them, our pupils excite our admiration by their gentleness and the respect they show not only to us, but to one another.

In scholarship they disappoint us. Their disadvantages we knew so well, so much had we heard of their inferiority, that we were unprepared to find them faithful, attentive, and quick of apprehension to such a degree as to place them on a level with scholars who had never known such disadvantages. Young men, who well remember when they were slaves, carried four studies (daily recitations) through a three months' term, and, upon the averaging of a carefully marked record, were found to have a rank above ninety per cent, while a member of them ranked above ninety-five. What significant facts are these!

In connection with these facts, indicating the usefulness of our efforts, and the favor with which God has regarded them, I can not forbear to mention the crying need of enlarged facilities, without which our work is painfully crippled. Our school-building has no plaster, paper, nor ceiling. In many places the light shines through its crevices. We could not keep it comfortably warm during the coldest weather. So confined are our accommodations that six young men occupy together a room only thirteen by twenty (13 x 20) feet square, deprived thus by necessity of the privacy which a student should have, and the retirement which is so necessary for prayer and meditation. By crowding them thus, their comfort, health, and progress are greatly interfered with. Though desirous to afford equal educational-privileges to the daughters of the people, on whom no less than on the sons depends the salvation and elevation of the race, our limited room does not permit it to be done.

We need this day a new building and improvements on the old costing not less than five thousand dollars—absolutely NEED it, not for show nor pride nor rivalry, but for Christ's poor, our brethren. This amount would furnish the simplest and cheapest space for a hundred more students. As much as many a Church would spend for a spire would open here a building which would make it possible for us to educate a hundred preachers and teachers next year, every one of whom would be a missionary. For which of these two purposes shall the Lord's money be used? Need I say to the thoughtful reader that now is the time to instruct and save this people, and so save the Church and the nation? It is the day of our most fearful need, the day of the people's peril.

The Centennial does not lay the cap-stone of the nation's life and glory. The foundations are still weak and the whole fabric trembling on account of the neglect and degradation of a great body of our citizens. The best contribution we can make to the year of celebration, as a thank-offering to God and a safeguard to our national existence, is to give ourselves or our money to evangelize and educate the colored people of the South. The nation fattened on their blood and toil, stood up in pride on their degradation, until, under the chastisement of Jehovah, it yielded back a portion of that blood, treasure, and pride in the war for freedom. But the debt will never be paid to the satisfaction of eternal justice until we deal as the "good Samaritan" with this wounded race; until we lift them up, bear them to the Christian school, where they may recover strength, pay for their temporary care, and promise more, should more be needed. Else, the robbers will again fall upon them, and their blood will God require at our hands.

NEW ORLEANS UNIVERSITY.

Rev. W. D. GODMAN, D. D., President.
A. B. COLLINS, Professor of Ancient Languages.
MRS. A. DEXTER GODMAN, M. D., Professor of Natural Science.
MISS. CLARA SALT, Professor of English Literature.
MRS. CLARA BENNETT, Professor of Music.

THIS institution is very eligibly located in the city of New Orleans, 459 Camp Street—the grounds fronting on Coliseum Square, one of the most pleasant parks in the city. It occupies two buildings—one for school purposes and the other for residence and a boarding-house. The members of the Faculty and a few students are accommodated in the buildings.

CONDITION AND PROSPECTS.

The New Orleans University has a commanding influence among our colored people, and a strong hold upon their confidence. It is *second* among schools of its class in New Orleans, as regards number of students, and would immediately take *first rank*, if its necessities were met by the Church. We solicit attention to the following statements—a prayerful and earnest attention from a Christian public.

1. There are hundreds (many hundreds) of colored youth,

many of them destined soon to graduate into the honors and responsibilities of citizenship, who are not educating themselves. Some have no interest in education, but might become interested through right instrumentalities. Many have not means to go to school, doomed to toil for support. *A moderate aid would bring such into the schools.*

2. But the New Orleans University, having now 110 students, has not room for more than twenty more. She can not accommodate that additional twenty for chapel worship, the largest room we now have being already inconveniently full.

3. Our building (the school building) is not in good repair, and is not worthy of much expense to put it in repair. The need is a *new building*.

4. Our location is beautiful, and the grounds are ample, when the old building shall be removed, for the erection of a *convenient and commodious University edifice*. Will not some man or woman, whose heart God has touched with love for his poor, give the Freedmen's Aid Society $25,000 for this holy purpose?

5. We have *no scientific apparatus* whatever. We feel deeply the need of this. We could make such apparatus, if we had it, a most effective instrument for building up the school.

Our library is very *meagre* in comparison with what it should be. Will not the mere statement of these facts stir up some of our Christian friends to help us?

6. We have a theological class of *eight*. Other institutions offer liberal aid to students for the ministry, and already they are reaping manifest advantages from the influence of those whom they send out. If we could command a scholarship fund of *two* to *three thousand dollars* annually, it would soon prove to be a most profitable investment for the Church. We have special contributions for this end to a small amount, but we should have many times more.

The Methodist Episcopal Church has had a grander opportunity than any other Protestant people. *She is not now improving it with the zeal and energy required.* A few years of this undecided, non-vigorous policy will bring us to great and unavailing regrets. By striking *now*, and using means liberally, we can secure and maintain the vantage-ground for all the future.

Special attention is given to *religious culture*. We have a daily *prayer-meeting*, of fifteen minutes' length, with our students, *besides* the regular daily chapel worship. Every Friday evening a meeting is held in a recitation-room for the promotion of *holiness*. Every Sabbath a Sunday-school is held in our building, which at present numbers 115 scholars.

HAVEN NORMAL SCHOOL.

Rev. C. W. M'Mahon, Principal.
Mrs. C. W. M'Mahon, Teacher.

This school is located in Central Eastern Georgia, in the town of Waynesboro, on the Augusta and Savannah railroad, and easily accessible by rail car, and every other mode of conveyance. This location is in the very heart of a large colored population, for whose mental and spiritual elevation this school is designed. Its chief work is to prepare and send forth teachers and preachers into all this region.

From twenty to forty miles around us, in every direction, this country swarms with colored people, and ours is the only school of any importance, designed for them, that exists in all this large territory—in fact, the *only* one of its kind. For several years this school has been working here with constantly increasing efficiency and influence, until now its influence with these masses is incalculably great. Our school numbers one hundred and thirty pupils, one-third of whom come from such a distance that they are obliged to board in the town; and this number of boarders is constantly increasing. The character of the school is also improving; for many of the pupils are young men and women of age and attainments; so that we have a normal school, not only in name, but in reality.

The greatest obstacle to our success is the want of a suitable school building. The building we use at present is one of the extremely uncomfortable churches which are so common in this country. It hardly need be said that such a building, uncomfortable, small, and every way unsuited to our work, is a serious hinderance to our progress. We have a building in process of erection that will meet our present necessities. It is sixty-six feet in length by thirty-eight in width, and three stories high. The first story (the basement) is designed for kitchen, dining-room, etc.; the second story, for main school-room, recitation-rooms, and hall; and the third story, for lodging-rooms, with attic above that. To erect this building and furnish it, we have pledges from our own people to the amount of $800; and we are striving with all our might to raise $1,000. We have pledges outside our own people that will be fully met, still we shall need at least $1,000; and we look to our friends of the Methodist Episcopal Church in the North, through Bishop Haven and the Freedmen's Aid Society, to assist us in raising this amount. Only think of the small amount to be raised, and then think of the *incalculable* good to be accomplished with it to the mass of colored people in this neglected portion of our common country; and God will make it easy for you to give us this pittance, and so firmly establish Haven Normal School that it may be a blessing here for all coming time.

RUST NORMAL INSTITUTE.

Mr. C. W. Munson,
Miss M. C. Owen, } Principals.

This Institute, located at Huntsville, Alabama, one of the healthiest and most beautiful cities of the South, has a twofold work to do—preparing young men and women for the greatest and noblest of professions, teaching and preaching. So far the work is of a preparatory nature, although many have gone out to teach and preach to the eager, hungry thousands.

The building is large, substantial, and convenient, and will accommodate two hundred and fifty, if necessary. What the colored people want, and must have, are teachers of their own color, who can go out among the people and do the work no one else can do. Nearly all the preachers teach school in connection with their Church work.

The school needs a teachers' home and conveniences for boarding students, all of which could be put into one building on the present roomy grounds. The class of students who are the most valuable, as a rule, live in the country, and there is very little to draw them in, as board is high, and accommodations uncertain. Will some good friend of these poor people donate $2,000 or $3,000, to make this a permanent monument of usefulness in the work God has for his Church to do among this Israel of bondage.

The grade of scholarship is good, there being a class reading "Cæsar," and studying "Ray's Higher Algebra;" but most of the school are in the common English branches.

BENNETT SEMINARY.

Rev. F. O. Thayer, A. B., Principal.

This institution, located at Greensboro, N. C., was organized under the auspices of the Freedmen's Aid Society in 1874. There is no question about the wisdom of establishing a school of the kind in this locality. The universal interest manifested by the people, and the evident demand that such educational advantages should be afforded, make it evident that soon this new enterprise will take high rank among our institutions. The place is well adapted to the growth of the school, being the seat of several institutions of learning, including the Female Seminary of the North Carolina Conference of the "Church South," and situated in the central part of the State, and on the direct line of railroad between Richmond and Atlanta, Georgia. During the Winter and Spring terms the average attendance of students was seventy-five, and ranging in age from fourteen to thirty years.

A beautiful site for the Seminary building, including twenty acres, has been purchased by the Freedmen's Aid Society, at a cost of twenty-two hundred dollars. It is situated in the suburbs of the city, commanding a view of the place, is healthy and easy of access.

The design of the patrons of the school is to erect suitable buildings upon this purchased ground, and there permanently locate the school, which has been conducted in the basement of the Methodist Episcopal Church. This building would have been commenced the present year, but for the *hard times*, which so materially affected the raising of funds for the purpose. It is to be hoped, however, that another year will see the buildings, so much needed for the school, completed. Let the friends of the freedmen aid this enterprise, and hasten the completion of the buildings by their increased contributions.

The prospect for this school in its future conduct, is every way encouraging. The people of the place, the preachers of the Conference, scattered as they are, all over the entire State, are deeply interested in the Seminary, and are doing all that they are able for its prosperity. A collection taken by the colored people of the Methodist Church in Greensboro amounted to *one hundred and five dollars*. This amount was made up of small contributions, the Sabbath-school children bringing their pennies, which, at the suggestion of their parents and pastor, they have been saving for this purpose. One little fellow, who had received a Sabbath-school prize of a dollar, brought it and placed it on this altar. This will convey to the reader an idea of the interest the people feel in the enterprise.

Little or no aid can be expected from the white people of the place, though many have expressed themselves to us as being glad such a school has been started. While most of the aid necessary for the maintenance of the school must come from the North, it is gratifying to feel that with the growth of the school the old prejudice of caste is abating. Let all be done that can for the freedmen. In no field is aid more needed, and nowhere will money loaned to the Lord bring quicker or larger returns.

CENTENARY BIBLICAL INSTITUTE.

Rev J. Emory Round, A. M., President.

This Institute, located at Baltimore, was organized December 25, 1866, under the supervision of Bishops Scott and Ames, who appointed the following Trustees: Thomas Kelso,

William Harden, William Daniel, William B. Hill, John Lanahan, Henry W. Drakeley, Hugh L. Bond, James H. Brown, Charles A. Reid, Isaac P. Cook, Francis A. Crook, Robert Turner and Samuel Hindes.

The sum of $5,000, from an appropriation by the Missionary Society of the Methodist Episcopal Church, for the education of colored preachers, was paid into its Treasury. The Institute was chartered by the Superior Court of Baltimore, November 27, 1867. The provisions of the charter are similar to that of Drew Theological Seminary. Candidates for admission are required to present recommendations from a quarterly conference, certifying that, in the opinion of the conference, the candidate is called of God to the ministry. The assent of at least two of the bishops is requisite to the validity of any change in the charter, of the course of study, or of the election of any instructor. All vacancies in the Board of Trustees are to be filled by the bishop who shall preside at the next session of the Baltimore Conference, on the nomination, by said Board, of twice the required number.

On the 19th of October, 1868, Rev. J. H. Brown, D. D., and Rev. William Harden were elected Professors. Under their direction, two sessions of the Institute were held; the first in the Fall and Winter of 1868–69, the second in 1869–70. They had two classes under their charge, to each of which they lectured once a week. One consisted of pastors laboring in Baltimore and vicinity, the other of local preachers. The arrangements to send to other schools such young men as could devote their time more steadily to study, continued till 1872.

In May, 1872, the Board, under the inspiration of the earnest appeals of Rev. R. S. Rust, D. D., Corresponding Secretary of the Freedmen's Aid Society of the Methodist Episcopal Church, and encouraged by the hearty and unanimous indorsement of the Baltimore Conference, at its previous session, purchased the building we now occupy, No. 44 Saratoga Street. On the 6th of September, the writer was elected to take charge of the work; and, on the 9th of October, the Institute was formally opened, with nine students.

During the first academic year we had thirty-two names on the rolls, but nearly two-thirds of them were married exhorters, local preachers, and others, whose attendance was quite irregular. All but one of them were either ministers, or candidates for the ministry recommended according to our charter. During the second year, forty were in attendance, thirty-five of whom were of the class contemplated by our charter.

At the beginning of our third academic year, it was determined to throw open all of the privileges of the Institute to young men of good moral character, likely to do good service in teaching, so far as it could be done without organizing additional classes, or depriving any of the students for the ministry of any facilities they might otherwise enjoy; with the further understanding that all students, not provided for in the charter, be required to pay a small charge for such privileges as they might receive.

The total number in attendance during the year is fifty-six, of whom thirty-five are either ministers or candidates for the ministry. Twenty-one are preparing to teach.

Twenty-eight members of annual conferences have received more or less of the benefits of our instruction since the Institute was organized, either before or since they entered the ministry. About forty others are in the local ministry. Twenty-three of our students are known to have done good service in teaching. None of them have completed our full normal course as yet, but all of them are qualified far better than the average of teachers employed in colored schools.

A more thorough training in elementary branches for both preachers and teachers is the most urgent necessity of the hour. The natural tendency, in all ignorant communities that aspire after improvement, is to acquire a superficial acquaintance with many books, without a real knowledge of any. In a certain sense, it would be easy to yield to this tendency; to make the past misfortunes of the race an excuse for a rapid, unsystematic, half-culture; to teach Latin and Algebra, after a certain fashion, to those who have an imperfect acquaintance with English Orthography and Long Division; to rush through book after book, and grade after grade; and, finally to confer degrees upon students who would scarcely be out of the Grammar School, but for the allowance which a sadly mistaken charity makes for their color.

COOKMAN INSTITUTE.

Rev. S. B. Darnell, Principal.
Mrs. S. B. Darnell, Teacher.

This institution is located at Jacksonville, Florida. It is engaged in preparing young men for the ministry, and both sexes for teachers. We have about fifty students, and applications for more than we can accommodate. There is no Biblical or Normal School for freedmen but this in the entire State. It extends four hundred miles north and south, and three hundred east and west; contains one hundred thousand people now to be reached, influenced, and blessed. They are ten years old in citizenship and manhood. Morally, intellectually, and financially, they are only beginning to live! The Freedmen's Bank has failed, and swept away the hopes of thousands. The schools are yet feeble and few. Northern teachers can not be sustained, colored are unqualified, though calls are coming in for those under our care who have been at school only a year. Preaching here is of a very inferior character. In numerous cases, " blind leaders of the blind " are they. Intelligent preaching is heard in the towns, but generally the ministers have never pursued a course of study; and were it not for the divine unction depended upon by the devout, degrading indeed would be the course advised and pursued.

The Freedmen's Aid Society has purchased a site, and our plan is for the first building, forty by sixty, three stories, and of brick. It will cost, when finished and furnished, ten thousand dollars. Our State and people are poor. Funds must come from the North to carry on this Christianizing power. The Treasury of the Freedmen's Aid Society is overdrawn. Its efforts span a mighty country, one thousand miles long and eight hundred wide. Its supplies were only $66,000, and this is doing as much as all the other societies for these five millions of uneducated American citizens. Help, help, is the cry coming up loud and strong! Heathendom has no such claims as these upon the charities of this lovely land! It comes to you through this. Do you not see the

Ethiopian stretching forth his hands unto God, in whose name I plead; and will you not put forth a special effort that will enable you to remit to Dr. Rust funds enough to erect our greatly needed building, in the center of population in the State?

GENERAL REMARKS.

HELP FOR POOR STUDENTS.

We earnestly plead for aid in behalf of a class of promising young men who, to all human appearance, are called of God to preach the unsearchable riches of Christ, and yet are too poor to meet the expenses of attending school. God not only calls young men to preach the Gospel, but also to make such preparation as may be necessary to discharge this duty intelligently and successfully; and if, in his wisdom, the selection is made from those in poverty and the humble walks of life, destitute of the means requisite to secure the advantages of education, it clearly becomes the duty of the Church to aid in this preparation. This seems to be in accordance with divine wisdom; for God selects a large proportion of those whom he designs to preach the Gospel, from the poor, that, in addition to other advantages, they may be prepared to bear the burdens and enter into the sympathies of the people—duties which those born in wealth and nursed in luxury would not be inclined to perform. But the early life of these young men prepares them for the deprivations and arduous duties of their calling.

There are hundreds of young men now in our schools, struggling to obtain an education preparatory to their entering the ministry, who will be compelled to abandon their studies, and give up in despair, unless they can receive some assistance. They are willing to do all they can to support themselves in school; but it is so difficult to obtain remunerative employment, that it is utterly impossible for them to attend school, make progress in their studies, and by their own exertions pay all their expenses. They must have some assistance to supplement their earnings. Fifty dollars a year will enable one of these theological students to continue his studies preparatory to the Christian ministry; and in some instances even twenty-five dollars will do it; and in view of the great demand for intelligent preachers, and the great good that such may accomplish among this people, we appeal to all who love Christ and his suffering poor, for aid in this work of educating our colored young men for the Christian ministry. One hundred of these are demanded to-day for our Southern work. Who will become responsible for the education of one of these students for the year, by the payment of fifty dollars, or even twenty-five? The person donating this money shall be furnished with the name of the beneficiary, and he can communicate with him from time to time, and ascertain his views, progress in study, and prospect of usefulness. The money can be forwarded to Rev. R. S. Rust, Cincinnati, O., the Corresponding Secretary, who will select the beneficiary, inform the donor of the selection, and furnish such information as may be desired.

The old plantation preachers did a good work in their time; but a more intelligent ministry, and one of purer morality, is now demanded for the instruction of this people, and for their preservation from the perils to which they are exposed. Preachers must be provided for this people who shall be able to expound the Scriptures, explain our doctrines, and defend the truth. The interests at stake are too momentous to be intrusted to ignorant ministers. The age in which we live, the field we cultivate, the character of the opposition which we encounter, the consequences involved, demand cultivated intellect, pure hearts, and holy enthusiasm in the Christian ministry.

OUR DEBT.

It will be observed that the Society is in debt eighteen thousand twenty-eight dollars and forty-six cents, incurred not in current expenses, for these have been kept within the annual collections, but in the investment of permanent school property, which will be remunerative for years to come. The Secretary, by authority of the Board of Managers, planned the operations of the Society for the year upon a careful estimate of its real income, and, by rigid economy and persistent effort, has kept the expenditures so nearly within this limit, that it was found necessary to make only the small loan of two hundred and forty-nine dollars fifty-seven cents, to meet the entire deficiency for the present year; the deficiency for last year being eight thousand and twelve dollars sixty-seven cents, and that of the year preceding nine thousand seven hundred and sixty-six dollars twenty-two cents, making the aggregate of indebtedness eighteen thousand twenty-eight dollars forty-six cents. When it is remembered that the urgency of this work has been so great, and the peril of delay so immense, no one, we think, will feel disposed to blame the Society for its indebtedness, especially as it has a property worth ten times its outstanding obligations, to meet any emergency or disaster.

One hundred thousand dollars was the sum estimated by the Board of Managers, after careful deliberation and examination, as the smallest amount demanded for the prosecution of this work among the freedmen, which has been intrusted to their care by the General Conference, for the current year. Only eighty-six thousand five hundred and sixty dollars and thirty-three cents have been raised; although it is a handsome increase over the income of the preceding year, yet it leaves a deficit on the estimate almost sufficient to liquidate the entire indebtedness against the Society.

A much larger than the estimated amount of one hundred thousand dollars should have been raised by a Church of so large a membership, and possessing so much wealth; but the varied benevolences of the Church were pressing their claims so urgently upon our people, that the Board of Managers did not deem it judicious to plan their work upon a more extensive scale, or apportion a larger sum to the Conferences. But every dollar of that apportionment should have been met, and might have been, had fidelity to the requirements of the Discipline been adhered to, and the claims of this cause earnestly presented to the people, and donations in its behalf solicited. Dear brethren of the ministry, will you perform this service for Christ and this poor people? If so, our debt shall speedily be paid, the necessary sum for another year shall be raised; and the enterprise of saving five millions of people, and making them tributary to the salvation of the world, shall be crowned with success.

FINANCIAL STATEMENT.

The Financial Statement for the year ending June 1, 1875, is as follows:

Cash in Treasury, June 1, 1874	$8 97
Contributed from May 31, 1874, to June 1, 1875	86,304 34
Loan	249 57
Total receipts	$86,562 88

Salary of Corresponding Secretary, postage, office and traveling expenses	3,769 66
Salary, traveling expenses, and postage of General Agent	2,553 37
Printing	571 98
Clerk hire	350 00
Furniture for schools and homes	950 00
Repairs on buildings	1,900 00
Insurance and interest	1,740 52

ENDOWMENTS—Central Tennessee College....$10,000 00
            Shaw University............ 1,370 00
            Clark University............ 6,000 00
                                    17,370 00

REAL ESTATE—New Hall, Nashville, Tenn.......... $8,000 00
            New Orleans, La........................ 1,500 00
            Greensboro, N. C....................... 2,157 00
            New Building, Clark University...... 1,200 00
            Cookman Institute...................... 600 00
            Haven Normal School.................. 100 00
            Ellijay Seminary, Ellijay, Ga......... 2,539 68
                                    16,096 68

Salaries and board of teachers and school expenses.	41,258 12
Balance in Treasury	2 55
Total disbursements	$86,562 88

The indebtedness against the Society is as follows:

Loan to balance account at the close of the present year	$249 57
Loan to balance account at the close of year, June 1, 1874	8,012 67
Loan to balance account at the close of year, May 1, 1873	9,766 22
Total indebtedness	$18,028 46

SUMMARY—ANNUAL DISBURSEMENTS.

First year, total Disbursements	$37,139 89
Second " " "	50,167 24
Third " " "	*93,513 50
Fourth " " "	*82,719 49
Fifth " " "	51,568 43
Sixth " " "	55,134 98
Seventh " " "	66,995 74
Eighth " " "	86,562 88
Total	$523,802 15

* Including appropriations from Freedmen's Bureau.

AMOUNTS RECEIVED

BY REV. L. HITCHCOCK, D. D., TREASURER OF THE METHODIST FREEDMEN'S AID SOCIETY

JUNE, 1874.

Ashland, Ky. Con., by W. A. Dotson	$4 00
Carthage, S. E. Ind. Con., by T. W. Jones	3 00
New Carlisle, Cin. Con., by C. H. Lawton	31 65
Marcellus, C. N. Y. Con., by T. H. Youngman	50 00
A member of Wyoming Con., by Bishop Haven, per Dr. Rust	5 00
Be Ne Volus, Cin. Con., by E. H. Field	25 00
H. Welton, Mich. Con.	5 00
Oxford, Cin. Con., by D. C. Vance	10 00
Lyman Bennett, Esq., Troy Con., by Dr. Rust	500 00
Spencer Chapel, Ironton, Ohio Con., by James Mitchell	37 00
Philadelphia Con., by J. Spilman	400 00
Total	$1,070 65

JULY, 1874.

Athens Station, O. Con., by W. T. Harvey	$16 00
Orville Circuit, N. O. Con., by P. Kelser	10 41
Union M. E. Church, Philadelphia Con., by Thos. F. Mason	25 30
Tuition and donations at Clark Theological Seminary, by J. W. Lee	398 35
South Greencastle, N. W. Ind. Con., H. A. Buchtel	14 35
Erie, Seventh Street M. E. Church, Erie Con., by D. Rutledge	22 86
Erie, Simpson Chapel, Erie Con., by D. Rutledge	8 29
New England Con., by J. P. Magee	1,641 45
Providence Con., by J. P. Magee	155 00
Maine Con., by J. P. Magee	117 04
Vermont Con., by J. P. Magee	5 19
An anonymous brother, Hopewell, Pittsburg Con., by G. H. Hood	230 00
Columbus Grove, C. O. Con., by B. J. Hoadley	10 00
Third Street Charge, Indianapolis, S. E. Ind. Con., by S. T. Gillet	13 31
Ottumwa, Iowa Con., by E. L. Schreiner, St. Louis Depository	1 00
Widow in Israel	5 00
Bequest of Franklin S. Skinner, deceased, New Haven, Conn., by Dr. Rust	2,000 00
Total	$4,673 55

AUGUST, 1874.

Wesley Chapel, Columbus, Ohio Con., by Dr. Rust	$76 00
Carthage Circuit, S. E. Ind. Con., by T. W. Jones	4 00
Rising Sun, S. E. Ind. Con., by E. A. Campbell	5 00
Vienna, S. E. Ind. Con., by J. S. Swope	5 00
Camden, N. Ind. Con., by H. Hill	5 00
Lyman Bennett, Esq., Troy Con., by Dr. Rust	1,000 00
Mt. Washington, Cin. Con., by M. Kauffman	10 50
Miami Charge, Cin. Con., by C. H. Kalbfus	1 00
Asbury, Cin., Cin. Con., by J. E. Gilbert	10 00
Syracuse, C. N. Y. Con., by D. W. C. Huntington	6 00
Kenton, O., C. O. Con., by D. Rutledge	21 00
Marseilles, Ohio, C. O. Con., by D. Rutledge	7 85
Mansfield, N. O. Con , by D. Rutledge	21 22
Erie, Penn., Erie Con., by D. Rutledge	2 00
Cleveland, O., Erie Con., D. Rutledge	23 00
Berea, O., N. O. Con., by D. Rutledge	40 50
Huntsville, O., C. O. Con., by D. Rutledge	20 95
Trinity, Cin., Cin. Con., by Dr. D. H. Moore	50 00
St. Paul, Cin., Cin Con., by Dr. C. H. Payne	196 50
Walnut Hills, Cin. Con., by W. L. Hypes	100 00
Madisonville, O., Cin. Con., E. T. Wells	50 00
Troy, O., Cin. Con., by J. T. Bail	12 20
Bethel Circuit, O., Cin. Con., by W. E. Hines	10 00
Christie, Cin., Cin. Con., by J. T. Johnson	60 35
Carthage, S. E. Ind. Con., by T. W. Jones	2 00
Fairmount, Cin., Cin. Con., by J. N. Irvin	5 00
Total	$1,745 07

Treasurer's Report.

SEPTEMBER, 1874.

Edinburg, S. E. Ind. Con., by R. Roberts	5 00
Central German Con. Col., by Treasurer	47 46
Cash at Vineyard Grove, by Dr. Rust	5 00
Dr. N. G. Ladd, Malden, Mass., N. E. Con., by Dr. Rust	20 00
Donations for Bishop Haven's Seminary, Wyoming Con., by Dr. Nelson	25 00
Detroit Con. Col., by Dr. Rust	309 03
Michigan Con. Col., by Dr. Rust	469 18
N. W. Ind. Con. Col., D. Handley, Treasurer	293 62
S. E. Ind. Con. Col., by W. M. Grubbs	239 00
Cin. Con. Col., by A. Bowers	513 50
S. W. Ger. Con. Col., by Treasurer	18 85
C. O. Con. Col., by Treasurer	513 04
Ind. Con. Col., by W. Puett, Treasurer	255 97
S. E. Ind. Con. Col. (balance), by W. M. Grubbs, Treasurer	20 77
S. E. Ind. Con. Col. (special), by W. Grubbs, Treas.	161 40
Iowa Con. Col. by S. S. Murphy, Treas.	207 73
Van Buren Circuit, N. Ind. Con., by A. C. Gerard	5 00
Total	**$3,109 55**

OCTOBER, 1874.

Des Moines Con., Col., by W. F. Laidley	$264 61
N. W. Iowa Con., Col., by Dr. Rust	17 05
N. W. Iowa Con. Col., Ann., by Dr. Rust	100 85
Upper Iowa Con. Col., by Dr. Rust	366 03
Upper Iowa Con Ann. Col., by Dr. Rust	203 00
Minn. Con. Col., by Dr. Rust	139 31
Minn. Con. Ann. Col., by Dr. Rust	30 86
Iowa Con. Ann. Col., by Dr. Rust	107 00
O. Con. Col., by L. F. Drake	787 31
Dublin, Ind., N. Ind. Con., by H. J. Ramey	8 35
N. W. Ger. Con. Col., by Treasurer	11 25
California Con. Col., by John B. Hill	88 00
Oregon Con. Col., by John B. Hill	41 25
Shelbyville, Tenn. Con., by W. B. Rippletoe	1 00
N. O. Con., by Dr. Rust	730 22
R. W. Sanger, by Dr. Rust	50 00
Hitchcock & Walden, Chicago, Ill.	2,111 06
Nelson & Phillips, New York, by Dr. Rust	870 44
Gillespie, S. Ill. Con., by T. A. Eaton	80
Washington-street, St. Louis, S. W. Ger. Con., by H. Pfaff	2 15
Brighton, S. Ill. Con., by W. Wallis	15 00
Vandalia, S. Ill. Con., by Jos. Harris	6 00
Jerseyville, S. Ill. Con., by F. L. Thomson	10 00
Southern Illinois Con., Col. by J. C. Baldridge	248 70
Illinois Con., Col. by W. R. Powers	361 35
Nebraska Con., Col. by G. S. Alexander	7 15
Widow in Israel, $100 and $5	105 00
Colorado Con., Col. by J. H. Beardsley	27 05
New England Con., by Dr. Rust	11 50
Vermont Con., by Dr. Rust	14 00
East Maine Con., by Dr. Rust	9 50
Maine Con., by Dr. Rust	42 00
Total	**$6,787 79**

NOVEMBER, 1874.

Rev. S. W. Coggeshall, Pocasset, Mass., Providence Con., by Dr. Rust	10 00
Second Church, Norwalk, Conn., New York East Con., by R. Jones	9 50
Mrs. S. E. Creighton, for Ladies' Itinerant Association of the O. Con., for the education of two young ladies at Nashville	50 00
Simpson Chapel, Muncie, North Ind. Con., by D. Rutledge	100 00
St. Paul, Cin., Cin. Con., by Dr. Rust	100 00
Vestal Charge, Wyoming Con., by J. B. Santee	6 00
Norwalk, N. O. Con., by E. Persons	40 00
William-street Charge, Delaware, C. O. Con., by T. C. O'Kane & Co.	144 00
Clinton, N. New York Con., by O. C. Cole	40 00
Medina Charge, N. O. Con., by B. J. Hondley	10 00
L. A. Rudisill, Tenn. Con.	3 00
Holston Con., Col. by H. Reed, Treasurer	25 70
Tennessee Con., Col. by C. W. Wood, Treasurer	23 00
Alabama Con., Col. by J. P. M'Gee, Treasurer	25

FREEDMEN'S AID SOCIETY. 47

Georgia Con., Col by S. D. Brown, Treasurer	54 20
Arcadia, O., C. O. Con., by D. Rutledge	12 60
Salem O., Pittsburg Con., by D. Rutledge	5 69
Tiffin, O., N. O. Con., by D. Rutledge	17 73
Total	$651 67

DECEMBER, 1874.

Akron, O., Erie Con., by Mrs. Russell	$106 75
London, O., O. Con., by Mrs. Russell	41 21
Monroeville Station, N. O. Con., by T. J. Gard	10 00
Newark Valley, Wyoming Con., by Dr. Rust	15 65
Fostoria, O., C. O. Con	100 00
Oberlin, N. O. Con., by J. R. Jewitt	3 00
West Salem, N. O. Con., by D. Rutledge	12 38
Tiffin, N. O. Con., by D. Rutledge	16 40
Nelson & Phillips, New York, by Dr. Rust	100 00
Green-street Charge, Piqua, Cin. Con., by J. Stephenson	40 00
Bellevue, N. O. Con., by F. M. Searles	25 00
Perkinsville, N. Ind. Con., by J. F. Rhoades	10 00
Lockington, Cin. Con., by C. J. Wells	5 00
Joseph Osborn, Delphos, C. O. Con	3 00
London, O. Con., by T. H. Monroe	32 50
Vermillion Ct., N. O. Con., by R. Wilcox	7 00
Bowling Green, C. O. Con., by L. M. Albright	13 00
Wm. Shaw, El Paso, C. Ill. Con	10 00
Milan, N. O. Con., by D. Rutledge	5 12
Quincy, C. O. Con., by D. Rutledge	6 75
Pemberton, C. O. Con., by D. Rutledge	4 48
Adrian, C. O. Con., by D. Rutledge	12 50
I. T. Hayman, Kane, Ky. Con	1 02
Richmond, N. Ind. Con., by H. Gillam	10 00
Christ Church, Pittsburg, Pittsburg Con., by Dr. Rust	58 89
Third-street, Camden, N. Jer. Con., by Dr. Rust	30 78
Brother Bryan, Philadelphia, Philadelphia Con., by Dr. Rust	5 00
St. Paul, Delaware, O. Con., by R. M. Manley	17 00
Nelson & Phillips, New York, by Dr. Rust	711 30
Erie Con., Col., in part, by A. D. Morton	749 46
Lima, C. O. Con., by D. Rutledge	51 40
Central New York Con., Col. by Miss M. A. Sharp	71 17
Total	$2,285 76

JANUARY, 1875.

Wyoming Con., Col. by Miss M. A. Sharp	$328 83
Grand Rapids, C. O. Con., by W. J. Hodges	14 00
Rev. H. Harpst, Ludlowville, C. N. Y. Con	3 00
Richard Harrison, Mt. Vernon. Ct., by O. Barnett	50 00
Mrs. Dr. Gray, Piqua, O., Cin. Con., for education of Cornelia Hayden, by James Stephenson	20 00
Findlay, O., C. O. Con., by D. Rutledge	31 31
Delaware, N. O. Con., by B. F. Bell	22 00
St. Paul's, Toledo, C. O. Con., by D. Rutledge	32 85
St. John's, Toledo, C. O. Con., by D. Rutledge	20 00
Broadway, Toledo, C. O. Con., by D. Rutledge	6 51
S. S. Barten, Toledo, C. O. Con., by D. Rutledge	11 06
East Toledo, C. O. Con., by D. Rutledge	6 25
Brighton, Toledo, O., C. O. Con., by D. Rutledge	12 50
West Liberty, Toledo, O., C. O. Con., by D. Rutledge	12 00
Spring Hill, Toledo, O., C. O. Con., by D. Rutledge	7 50
Saranac, Mich., Michigan Con., by H. L. Brockway	6 95
Weston, C. O. Con., by A. C. Barnes	8 00
Rev. L. T. Clark, C. O. Con., by D. Rutledge	15 00
Pleasant Grove, O., Pittsburg Con., by D. Rutledge	8 75
Huntsville, O., C. O. Con., by D. Rutledge	6 25
Findlay, O., C. O. Con., by D. Rutledge	9 25
Melmore Ct., N. O. Con., by E. Y. Warner	5 32
E. Hinds, Long Island, N. Y. E. Con	1 00
Columbus Grove, C. O. Con., by G. Matthews	10 00
Carey Ct., C. O. Con., by J. Wykes	15 50
Mt. Auburn Church, from S. M. Y. Whetstone, Cin. Con., by J. N. Irvin	100 00
Total	$ 763 83

FEBRUARY, 1875.

Mrs. M. Ferree	5 00
M'Comb Ct., O. Con., by D. Rutledge	26 25
Bluffton, O. Con., by D. Rutledge	12 00
Van Wert Ct., O. Con., by D. Rutledge	9 00
Defiance, O. Con., by D. Rutledge	10 41
Middlepoint, O. Con., by D. Rutledge	17 00
Rev. E. Savage, Berea, O., N. O. Con., by J. S. Broadwell	80 00
Cairo, Detroit Con., by W. P. Maywood	3 00
Anna, C. O. Con., by J. R. Colgan	16 00
Fredericktown Ct., O. Con., by D. Rutledge	18 00
Napoleon, O. Con., by D. Rutledge	3 50
New Carlisle Ct., Cin. Con., by J. G. Black	6 00
Mrs. S. A. Joiner, Milledgeville Ct., North Carolina Con., by Dr. Rust	10 00
Louisiana Con. Col. by J. S. Leavitt	156 45
Erie Con., in part, by A. D. Morton	20 00
Lyman Bennett, Esq., Troy, Troy Con., by Dr. Rust	300 00
St. Paul's M. E. Church, Hazleton, Penn., C. Penn. Con., by W. W. Evans	22 00
Texas Con., by W. R. Fayle	41 10
Dr. C. K. True, N. Y. E. Con., by Dr. Rust	10 00
Southern German Con., by W. Pfaffe	2 00
Martinsville, Ind. Con., by S. L. Binkley	10 00
Pittsburg Con., in part, by James Horner	60 39
Trinity, Shelbyville, Ky. Con., by J. D. Walsh	6 00
Dr. Rust, personal donation by Dr. Hitchcock, Treasurer	300 00
Huntsville, C. O. Con., by D. Rutledge	16 00
Bryan Station, C. O. Con., by W. Deal	15 00
Be Ne Volus	5 00
Defiance, O. Con., by D. Rutledge	7 00
Arcadia, O. Con., by D. Rutledge	33 70
A. Brown, Columbus, O. Con., by D. Rutledge	100 00
A friend, Wyoming Con., by Dr. Nelson	200 00
Bloomfield, Ind. Con., by T. D. Welker	4 00
Mrs. Eliza Chrisman, for Clark University Endowment Fund by Bishop Haven	1,000 00
Corcord Ct, Ky. Con., by D. Akin	5 00
H. Bouck (personal), N. New York Con., by L. B. Gray	10 00
Cedar Lake, N. New York Con., by L. B. Gray	5 50
Joseph Osborn, Delphos, C. O. Con., self	2 00
Fletcher Place M. E. Church, Indianapolis, Ind., S. E. Ind. Con., by G. L. Curtiss	39 85
A friend, N. Ind. Con., by R. F. Brewington	2 00
Rev. O. Pearce, N. O. Con., by D. Rutledge	14 25
Rev. T. B. M'Clain, S. E. Ind. Con., by D. Rutledge	12 58
Port Clinton Sunday-school, C. O. Con., by D. Rutledge	6 00
Clyde, N. O. Con., by D. Rutledge	10 00
"C," Marseilles, C. O. Con	10 00
Nelson & Phillips, New York, by Dr. Rust	192 19
Xenia, N. Ind. Con., by J. S. Sellers	5 00
R. B. Pope, C. O. Con., by Miss Owen	100 00
L. W. Tulleys, Ottumwa, Iowa Con., by Dr. Hitchcock	100 00
Charles Palmer, Mansfield, N. O. Con	5 00
Prairie du Chien, W. Wis. Con., by G. W. Nuzum	3 40
Seargeant's Bluff, N. W. Iowa Con., by S. L. Burrill	40
Randolph Station, Wis. Con., by Jno. W. Olmstead	10 00
J. W. Agard. C. Ill. Con., self	10 00
Monticello, Minn. Con., by D. Brooks	5 29
Evanston, Second Church, Rock River Con., by W. Stonehouse	8 93
Chatfield, Minn. Con., by H. C. Jennings	6 00
Mrs. E. B. Russell, Agent	76 95
Michigan-avenue, Chicago, Rock River Con., by B. I. Hitchcock	45 90
Moline, C. Ill. Con., by W. M. Collins	6 00
Milford, C. Ill. Con., by A. Beeler	3 35
Mrs. E. B. Russell, Agent	58 65
Waverly, Upper Iowa Con., by J. H. Elliott	3 50
Deer Creek, C. Ill. Con., by J. A. Windsor	2 50
Rochester, Minn. Con., by H. P. Satchwell	10 25
Total	**$3,295 29**

MARCH, 1875.

A. Brobst, Philadelphia, Phila. Con., by W. T. Perkins	$10 00
Orphans' Home, by J. C. Hartzell	75 00
J. T. Hayman, Kane, Ky. Con	1 02
Fredericktown, N. O. Con., by P. D. Jones	5 00
Maumee City, C. O. Con., by D. Rutledge	18 00

FREEDMEN'S AID SOCIETY. 49

Ashland, Ky. Con., by W. A. Dotson	13 00
Yellow Springs, Cin. Con., by G. C. Crum	1 10
Galesburg, C. Ill. Con., by S. W. Brown	10 00
Lima Ct., O. Con., by D. Rutledge	10 00
"H. C. M."	5 00
Rev. S. P. Shaw, Bucyrus, N. O. Con	10 00
E. Remington, Esq., by Dr. Rust	50 00
Trinity M. E. Church, Indianapolis, Ind., Ind. Con., by J. H. Bayliss	73 00
Yellow Springs, Cin. Con., by G. C. Crum	5 90
Mrs. Crawford and Miss Wooden, Marshall, Ill. Con., by A. T. Orr	10 00
Wesley Chapel, Columbus, O. Con., by S. A. Keen	80 00
Roberts Park, Indianapolis, Ind., S. E. Ind. Con, by G. D. La Matyr and J. W. Ray	119 80
Philadelphia, Phila. Con., a poor woman's mite	10 00
Mary E. Fry, Newtown, O., Cin. Con	3 00
Dalton, N. O. Con., by T. Struggles	27 00
Apple Creek, N. O. Con., by P. Kelser	12 35
Plymouth, N. W. Ind. Con., by J. C. Stephens	6 00
West Virginia Con., Col. by A. J. Lyda, Treasurer	101 90
Meridian-street, Indianapolis, Ind. Con., by J. Taylor Treasurer	108 23
W. J. Baine, M. D., Fayette, Mich., Detroit Con	25 00
Olena Ill., C. Ill. Con., by T. P. Henry	11 00
Delavan, Ill., Ill. Con., by M. A. Howes	31 90
W. C. DePauw, New Albany, Ind. Con., by Dr. Rust	100 00
Medina, N. O. Con., by B. J. Hoadley	10 00
Brookston, N. W. Ind. Con., by D. Dale	12 00
Central New York Con., Col. by R. D. Phillips	46 00
Rev. E. Savage, Berea, O., N. O. Con., by J. S. Broadwell	120 00
Brunswick, N. O. Con., by A. P. Jones	20 00
Pleasant Hill, N. W. Ind. Con., by J. E. Wright	8 25
Grace Church, Indianapolis Ind., S. E. Ind. Con., by G. P. Jenkins	16 00
Kansas Con., Col. by J. D. Knox, Treasurer	11 90
Mechanicsville, N. Y., Troy Con., by G. C. Morehouse	23 00
Grand Rapids, Wis. Con., by Jesse Cole	10 00
Raper Church, Dayton, Cin. Con., by W. A. Robinson	56 00
Union Covington, Ky. Con., by J. S. Chadwick	60 65
Kentucky Con., Col. by T. S. Cowden, Treasurer	134 75
Lexington Con., by Dr. Reid	16 69
Nashville Circuit, Mich. Con., by E. L. Kellogg	5 00
Brookston, N. W. Ind. Con., by I. Dale	8 00
E. B. Youmans, Ky. Con., by self	5 90
Georgetown, Cin. Con., by J. P. Porter	11 10
Carbon, N. W. Ind. Con., by D. S. Morrison	5 00
Kalida, C. O. Con., by John Parlett	6 00
Twelve-mile Grove, Rock River Con., by Wm. Craven	13 10
Marion, C. O. Con., by D. Rutledge	50 20
Wellington, N. O. Con., by D. Rutledge	100 00
Nelson & Phillips, New York, by Dr. Rust	800 00
Tyrone, C. O. Con., by D. Rutledge	35 00
N. F. Tower, Ken. Con	2 00
Catlettsburg, Ky. Con., by E. L. Shepard	5 00
Brooklyn, N. O. Con., by A. Holbrook	33 00
Pelton Avenue Mission, Cleveland, N. O. Con., by H. L. Parrish	3 70
Kentucky Con., by T. S. Cowden, Treasurer	6 00
Total	$2,567 44

APRIL, 1875.

Nelson & Phillips, New York, by Dr. Rust	500 00
Asbury, Cin., Cin. Con., by J. E. Gilbert	$50 00
Sioux City Charge, N. W. Iowa Con., by J. A. Potter	10 00
Attica, N. W. Ind. Con., by Samuel Godfrey	4 50
Walkerton, N. W. Ind. Con., by D. Handley	3 00
Sycamore, N. O. Con., by J. S. Cutler	18 00
Brooklyn Station, Iowa Con, by W. G. Wilson	5 20
Mrs. Mary Morrison, Delaware, O. Con	15 00
German M. E. Church, Marion, C. O. Con., by D. Rutledge	5 00
Rushsylvania, C. O. Con., by D. Rutledge	4 70
Hopewell, O., Pittsburg Con., by D. Rutledge	11 45
Bellefontaine Ct., Iowa Con., by J. M. Mann	5 00
Gallipolis, O. Con., by C. D. Battelle	21 25
Wesley Webster, South Charleston	20 00
Forester Station, Detroit Con., by C. Gibbs	5 00
East Troy, Wis. Con., by Thomas Peep	2 20
Logan, O. Con., by J. F. Williams	16 35
North Indiana Con., Col. by S. J. M'Elwee	411 35
Oxford, N. W. Ind. Con., by D. G. Le Sourd	7 75
A widow, Lafayette, N. W. Ind. Con., by J. W. Joyce	5 00

Greene, Erie Con., by Z. W. Shaddock	10 00
Mt. Sterling, O. Con., by S. Rankin	6 00
Galena, N. O. Con., by W. B. Farrah	26 68
J. G. Baldwin, Middletown, Conn., N. Y. East Conn., by Dr. Rust	50 00
A friend at Boston, by Dr. B. K. Pierce, per Dr. Rust	16 00
A friend at Keokuk, by Bishop Haven, per Dr. Rust	20 00
Mrs. Edward Sargent, to furnish a room in Central Tennessee College, to be named for Mrs. A. B. Leonard	35 00
Nelson & Phillips, New York, by Dr. Rust	2,500 00
Rev. G. W. Stearns, Providence Con., by Dr. Rust	5 00
Rev. S. W. Coggeshall, Providence Con., by Dr. Rust	10 00
Mr. R. D. Kirky, N. Y. East Con., by Dr. Rust	50
Rev. Mr. Field, N. Y. East Con., by Dr. Rust	2 00
Edward Anthony, New Bedford, Providence Con., by Dr. Rust	25 00
Thomas W. Price, Philadelphia Con., by Dr. Rust	100 00
Cookman Institute, Newark Con., by Dr. Rust	30 00
Gilson, C. Ill. Con., by L. B. Dennis	7 00
Brother Souders, Central Church, Phila. Con., by W. Prettyman	45 00
Ebenezer, Phila. Con., by J. Spilman	147 97
Sylvania, Phila. Con., by J. Spilman	32 26
Central, Phila. Con., by J. Spilman	211 28
Hancock-street, Phila. Con., by J. Spilman	50 50
St. George's, Phila. Con., by J. Spilman	60 00
Columbia, Phila. Con., by J. Spilman	116 32
Marietta, Phila. Con., by J. Spilman	22 25
Spring Garden, Phila. Con., by J. Spilman	224 23
Kensington, Phila. Con., by J. Spilman	200 00
Cohocksink, Phila. Con., by J. Spilman	30 00
Nazareth, Phila. Con., by J. Spilman	57 15
Scott's, Phila. Con., by J. Spilman	76 50
Grace, Phila. Con., by J. Spilman	122 00
Centenary, Phila. Con., by J. Spilman	6 50
Tabernacle, Phila. Con., by J. Spilman	86 72
St. John's, Phila. Con., by J. Spilman	120 00
Wharton Street, Phila. Con., by J. Spilman	200 00
Nineteenth Street, Phila. Con., by J. Spilman	27 00
Frankfort Street, Phila. Con., by J. Spilman	50 00
Emory, Phila. Con., by J. Spilman	12 00
Small collections, Phila. Con., by J. Spilman	30 00
New England Con. Col. for North Carolina, by W. J. Parkinson	400 00
Swartz Creek, Detroit Con., by E. H. Brockway	7 50
H. R. Hamlin, Sabina. Cin. Con., by F. S. Hoyt	5 00
Gillespie, S. Ill. Con., by T. A. Eaton	4 55
Jerseyville, S. Ill. Con., by F. L. Thompson	20 00
Rolla, St. Louis Con., by I. J. K. Lunbeck	1 00
Union Church, St. Louis, St. Louis Con., by H. Schureman	28 97
Arkansas Con., Col. by I. G. Pollard	2 70
St. Louis Con., Col. by W. E. Wilson	24 58
Missouri Con., Col. by W. H. Bassett	69 05
M. W. Adcock	2 00
Total	$6,486 96

MAY, 1875.

A friend in New Jersey, Philadelphia, Phila. Con., by G. Hughes	2 00
J. C. Brook, Walnut Hills, Cin. Con., by Dr. Rust	12 00
Tennesseeans, by Dr. Rust	1,000 00
Metamora, S. E. Ind. Con., by G. L. Alder	5 00
J. P. Waterhouse, Cin. Con.	50 00
Ansonia, C. O. Con., by F. C. Wiltsee	10 00
Mechanicsville, Upper Iowa Con., by S. C. Freen	10 00
H. W. P. Allen, Turin, N. Y., N. N. Y. Con	8 00
H. Warner, Perrysburg, C. O. Con	10 00
Bequest of Rev. Jesse Harriman, Bangor, Mapen A. Prince, Ex'r, E. Maine Con	42 66
Otego, Wyoming Con., by D. Rutledge	20 00
Hudson-avenue, Albany, N. Y., Troy Con., by D. Rutledge	10 00
North Pearl-street, Albany, N. Y., Troy Con., by D. Rutledge	5 00
Grace Church, Albany, N. Y., Troy Con., by D. Rutledge	1 00
A friend, by D. Rutledge	1 00
Plainfield, N. J., N. Jer. Con., by Dr. Rust	10 00
First M. E. Church, Urbana, O., Cin. Con., by D. Rutledge, per G. M. Russell	77 00
East Union Ct., N. O. Con., by T. G. Roberts	21 15
Rev. Dr. Hatfield, Phila. Con., by Dr. Rust	100 00
Avon Ct., N. O. Con., by E. H. Dissette	5 00
Tuition at Rust Normal School	186 55
Tuition at Shaw University	175 25
Sale of land at Holly Springs, Miss	380 00

FREEDMEN'S AID SOCIETY. 51

Tennesseeans, by Dr. Rust	1,000 00
Greensboro, N. C., collection for land, by Rev. M. Parkinson	105 00
Peoria Ct., Iowa Con., by B. F. Shane	6 85
Pittsburg Con., Col. by Dr. J. Horner	1,197 36
Oxford, Cin. Con., by D. C. Vance	12 00
Nelson & Phillips, New York, by Dr. Rust	1,200 00
Trinity M. E. Church, Cin. Con., by Dr. D. H. Moore	110 00
Central M. E. Church, Springfield, Cin. Con., by E. M. Wells	131 20
Central Tennessee College, by Dr. Braden	3,020 18
Carthage, S. E. Ind. Con., by T. W. Jones	5 00
Norwalk Ct., Desmoines Con., by D. Le Mont	10 00
Paul-street, Frankford, Phila. Con., by J. Spilman	50 00
Cohocksink, Phila. Con., by J. Spilman	47 00
Columbia Phila. Con., by J. Spilman	63 00
Lancaster, Phila. Con., by J. Spilman	60 00
Ebenezer, Phila. Con., by J. Spilman	101 00
Nineteenth-street, Phila. Con., by J. Spilman	10 00
Manayunk, Phila. Con., by J. Spilman	11 00
Norristown, Phila. Con., by J. Spilman	15 00
Olivesburg Ct., N. O. Con., by J. M'Nabb	31 00
Grace M. E. Church, Dayton, O., Cin. Con., by Dr. Pearne	150 13
Providence Con., by J. P. Magee	851 52
New England Con., (in part) by J. P. Magee	768 92
New Hamshire Con., (in part) by J. P. Magee	523 22
Maine Con., (in part) by J. P. Magee	269 16
East Maine Con., by J. P. Magee	192 11
Vermont Con., by J. P. Magee	249 74
Golconda, Ill. C. Ger. Con., by F. A. Hoff	3 00
Nelson & Phillips, New York, by Dr. Rust	2,142 95
Rev. Dr. Hatfield, Phila. Con., by Dr. Rust	500 00
Dr. Rust, personal donation. Clark University Endowment Fund by Dr. Hitchcock	1,900 00
Hugh Meharry, Shawnee Mound, Ind., for Endowment Fund of Central Tennessee College, by Dr. Braden	10,000 00
Gov. Wm Claflin, Boston, New Eng. Con., by Dr. Cooke	500 00
Mrs. George Harvey, Saratoga, Troy Con., by Dr. Cooke	10 00
Tuition and donation at Claflin University, by Dr. Cooke	376 00
Sunday-school Union, (in books) by C. O. Edwards, Treasurer	500 00
Mississippi Con., Col. by Dr. M'Donald	102 75
Philadelphia Con., (in part) by J. B. M'Cullough	812 08
Courtland, C. N. Y. Con., by J. Alabaster	20 00
Tennesseeans, by Dr. Rust	800 00
Bequest of H. H. Keator, deceased, by R. Bernard, Ex'r	1,000 00
Metamora and Eureka, C. Ill. Con., by A. C. Price	1 00
Monmouth, C. Ill. Con., by Levi E. Ohler	10 00
Monticello, Minn. Con., by J. G. Teter	6 00
Mrs. E. M. Hagans, to educate H. C. Dennis and F. M. Gordon at Clark University	50 00
Peotone, Rock River Con., by D. L. Christian	13 00
Ft. Atkinson, Wis. Con., by H. Colman	15 00
Marion, Upper Iowa Con., by S. A. Lee	13 50
Waukesha, Wis. Con., by S. Halsey	11 00
Mankato, Centenary Charge, Minn. Con., by J. Door	5 00
Smithville, C. Ill. Con., by T. Hoagland	4 50
Edgington, C. Ill. Con., by W. H. Campbell	5 00
Wyoming, C. Ill. Con., by J. W. Agard	10 00
Farmington, Minn. Con., by Thos. Day	4 00
Grant Place, Rock River Con., by T. C. Clendening	12 76
Davenport, Upper Iowa Con., by T. M'Clary	22 00
Prempton, C. Ill. Con., by Thos. Watson	6 00
Cameron, C. Ill. Con., by N. T. Allen	4 00
Frankfort Station, Rock River Con., by W. H. Strout	20 50
Sibley, N. W. Iowa Con., by Ira Brashears	5 00
Rooks Creek, C. Ill. Con., by L. N. Webber	2 50
Landon, Upper Iowa Con., by A. M. Smith	4 00
Frankfort Station, Rock River Con., by W. H. Strout	50
Elk Grove Ct., Rock River Con., by G. C. Clark	4 00
Roseville, C. Ill. Con., by J. W. Coe	5 00
Walden, Rock River Con., by R. Congdon	3 00
Oak Park, Rock River Con., by W. D. Atchison	23 50
Seneca, C. Ill. Con., by B. V. Denning	5 20
Princeton, Rock River Con., by W. H. Glass	15 00
Rock Island, C. Ill. Con., by W. C. Knapp	35 00
DeKalb, Rock River Con., by O. F. Mattison	12 25
Winona, C. Ill. Con., by W. A. Spencer	15 50
Greenbush, Wis. Con., by R. Blackburn	2 00
Cornell, C. Ill. Con., by J. W. Denning	4 00
Lansing, Mich. Con., by A. A. Knappen	12 42
Deer Creek, C. Ill. Con., by J. A. Windsor	2 60
Pleasant Mount, C. Ill. Con., by W. H. Hitchcock	3 00

TREASURER'S REPORT.

Dixon, Rock River Con., by I. Linebarger	15 00
Oird, Mich, Con., by Jas. Hamilton	12 50
Mt. Morris, Rock River Con., by E. M. Battis	10 00
Minneapolis, Washington-avenue, Minn. Con., by J. T. Lewton	10 00
Albion, Mich. Con., by L. Tarr	11 13
Rockford, Rock River Con., by Wm. Aug. Smith	5 30
Constantine, Mich. Con., by L. M. Edmonds	11 00
New Rutland, C. Ill. Con., by T. M. Dunham	4 00
Lyons, Upper Iowa Con., by J. S. Eberhart	5 75
State-street, Chicago, Rock River Con., by N. M. Stokes	4 00
Central City, Upper Iowa Con., by R. Ricker	20 00
Ellison Ct., C. Ill., Con., by E. Ransom	7 00
Rockford, Rock River Con., by Wm. Aug. Smith	13 00
Postville, Upper Iowa Con., by J. L. Paine	11 30
St. Paris and Lena, Cin Con., by J. Pearson	48 00
Rev. David Rutledge, personal donation, by Dr. Rust	85 00
Bellefontaine, C. O. Con., by D. Rutledge	69 65
Delphos, C. O. Con., by D. Rutledge	14 00
Lima, C. O. Con., by D. Rutledge	2 50
Wm. Fisher, M. D., Pikesville, Md., Balt. Con., by Rev. J. Round	100 00
J. Fisher, M. D., Pikesville, Md., Baltimore Con., by J. Round	100 00
Thomas Kelso, Balt., Md., Balt. Con., by J. Round	50 00
F. A. Crook, Balt., Md., Balt. Con., by J. Round	25 00
Joshua Regester, Balt., Md., Balt. Con., by J. Round	25 00
William B. Hill, Balt., Md., Balt. Con., by J. Round	25 00
Summerfield Baldwin, Balt., Md., Balt. Con., by J. Round	25 00
William Daniel, Balt., Md., Balt. Con., by J. Round	20 00
B. F. Bartlett, Balt., Md., Balt. Con., by J. Round	20 00
William Fuller, Balt., Md., Balt. Con., by J. Round	20 00
F. W. Heath, Balt., Md., Balt. Con., by J. Round	20 00
L. H. Cole, Balt., Md., Balt. Con., by J. Round	10 00
B. F. Bennett, Balt., Md., Balt. Con., by J. Round	10 00
German B. Hunt, Balt., Md., Balt. Con., by J. Round	10 00
Baltimore Con., (additional) by J. Round	512 22
Washington Con	234 13
Delaware Con	87 47
Wilmington Con	386 08
Tuition at Centenary Institute	83 25
For students at Centenary Institute	200 00
Sharp-street Church, Balt., Washington Con	8 00
Zoar Church, Phila., Delaware Con	30 00
New Hampshire Con., Col. by Dr. E. Adams	231 42
Mrs. Lee Claflin, by Dr. Cooke	150 00
South Kansas Con., Col. by S. Holman	40 53
State Funds for Normal School, Huntsville, Ala	250 00
New Orleans University, by Prof. Leavitt	915 97
State Funds for Preparatory-school at Atlanta, Ga., by Dr. Fuller	2,200 00
Haven Normal School, by C. W. M'Mahon	320 15
Endowment Fund of Shaw University, by Dr. M'Donald	1,970 00
Aid of students at Shaw University, by Dr. M'Donald	250 00
Mrs. Bishop Clark, for Clark University Endowment Fund, by Bishop Haven	1,000 00
W. C. DePauw, for Clark University Endowment Fund, by Bishop Haven	1,000 00
E. Remington, Ilion, N. Y., for Clark University Endowment Fund, by Bishop Haven	1,000 00
Bishop Haven, for Clark University Endowment Fund, by Dr. Rust	1,000 00
Tuition and donations for students at Clark University, by I. J. Lansing	600 00
Dr. A. C. M'Donald, Miss. Con., by Dr. Rust	100 00
J. T. Hayman, Kane, Ky. Con	1 02
Mechanicsburg, Cin. Con., by W. Fitzgerald	84 10
Rent at Shaw University, by W. W. Hooper	526 20
New Building at Nashville, Tenn	9,000 00
Total	$52,866 78

SUMMARY.

June	$1,070 65	December	$2,285 76
July	4,673 55	January	763 85
August	1,715 07	February	3,295 29
September	3,109 55	March	2,507 41
October	6,787 79	April	6,486 96
November	651 67	May	52,866 78
Total			$86,004 31

CONFERENCE COLLECTIONS.

From the General Minutes of 1875 we find the annual conferences donated to the Freedmen's Aid Society, through their pastors, in the annual collections, the following sums, arranged in accordance with the amount thus raised by the seventy-seven conferences:

CONFERENCES.	Amount	No. pastoral charges	No. taking collections	No. not taking collections	Amount per member
Cincinnati	$4,885 29	119	88	31	.149
Philadelphia	2,830 81	216	102	114	.073
New England	2,297 00	211	117	94	.085
Indiana	1,712 08	109	59	50	.056
Central Ohio	1,647 76	115	94	21	.076
Troy	1,607 33	211	151	60	.052
Rock-river	1,556 40	201	146	55	.065
North Ohio	1,518 14	112	97	15	.071
Wyoming	1,364 57	173	164	9	.056
Pittsburg	1,299 92	237	128	109	.024
Central New York	1,185 00	213	176	37	.039
Erie	1,152 10	233	168	65	.030
Providence	1,092 89	176	110	66	.058
Central Pennsylvania	1,085 15	162	111	51	.034
Ohio	1,049 46	136	104	32	.028
New Jersey	992 28	170	123	47	.034
New York East	942 85	243	82	161	.024
Baltimore	920 22	123	58	65	.031
Northern New York	903 00	175	142	33	.040
Upper Iowa	881 70	153	125	28	.043
New York	836 73	237	96	141	.021
Newark	802 00	201	109	92	.025
West New York	794 87	180	152	28	.043
Central Illinois	781 83	186	160	26	.029
Michigan	733 84	218	136	82	.030
New Hampshire	652 82	125	78	47	.052
South-eastern Indiana	582 30	92	76	16	.022
Illinois	578 00	206	116	90	.015
Wisconsin	541 39	145	117	28	.038
Iowa	535 72	106	94	12	.028
Mississippi	521 10	128	39	89	.019
North Indiana	490 33	142	113	29	.019
Detroit	457 49	199	82	117	.021
Maine	429 61	118	60	58	.036
Des Moines	428 32	127	75	52	.024
North-west Indiana	406 78	119	84	35	.017
Vermont	352 62	122	65	57	.036
Minnesota	342 81	149	92	57	.028
Wilmington	336 05	100	49	51	.014
Kentucky	234 80	84	34	50	.014
Southern Illinois	219 92	131	84	47	.009
East Maine	188 99	92	54	38	.022
West Wisconsin	186 95	109	60	49	.017

CONFERENCE COLLECTIONS.

CONFERENCES.	Amount.	No. pastoral charges.	No. taking collections.	No. not taking collections.	Amount per member.
California	$156 50	136	31	105	.019
Louisiana	156 45	75	45	30	.016
East Oregon and Washington	145 45	29	6	23	.018
Central German	137 58	84	41	43	.011
South Kansas	125 28	83	35	48	.013
West Virginia	104 30	110	49	61	.004
Tennessee	91 55	80	42	38	.009
East German	85 75	39	24	15	.027
Washington	79 52	103	26	77	.003
Georgia	79 35	97	35	62	.006
Missouri	66 45	117	45	72	.004
South-west German	63 50	110	31	79	.006
St. Louis	57 09	138	41	97	.004
Colorado	54 60	34	25	9	.020
North-west Iowa	52 04	65	30	35	.012
South Carolina	47 35	100	30	70	.001
Oregon	44 55	44	15	29	.013
Texas	41 10	80	30	50	.003
Chicago German	32 10	54	8	46	.006
Nebraska	30 02	101	22	79	.003
Alabama	29 25	83	5	78	.002
Holston	28 70	86	23	63	.001
North-west German	23 75	55	14	41	.005
Delaware	23 15	51	21	30	.002
Kansas	19 60	96	9	87	.002
North Carolina	13 85	45	15	30	.001
Virginia	11 93	43	11	32	.002
Florida	8 90	32	9	23	.004
West Texas	8 80	54	8	46	.001
Arkansas	7 05	41	14	27	.001
Lexington	6 60	40	7	33	.001
Rocky Mountains	4 75	30	3	27	.008
Southern German	2 00	20	4	16	.003
Nevada		15			
Total reported from conferences	$44,198 08	9,174	5,124	4,050	
Amount which went directly to the Treasurer of the Freedmen's Aid Society, irrespective of Conference boundaries, and was not reported in the General Minutes.	42,106 26				
Total collections as per Treasurer's report.	86,304 34				.062

It will be seen by the above that, during the year reported, only a little more than one-half of the pastoral charges took the collection for the Freedmen, ordered by the General Conference. If all of them had taken the collection, after a faithful presentation of the claims of this cause, every dollar of the *one hundred thousand dollars* apportioned to the conferences by the Board of Managers would have been raised.

In behalf of the Board of Managers,

R. S. RUST, Corresponding Secretary.

Anniversary of the Freedmen's Aid Society.

This was held Thursday evening, December 2, 1875, at the Metropolitan Church, Washington, D. C.

The opening religious exercises were conducted by Rev. J. A. Lansing, of Nashville, Tenn. Rev. Dr. Newman, presided, and introduced the exercises with a pertinent speech in which he referred to the providence of God in emancipating the slaves, and in the formation of this Society, which had accomplished so grand a work in the education of this race. He portrayed the wants of Africa, the grandeur of this mission, and urged the Society to give especial attention to the work of preparing young men for the redemption of that benighted land.

Dr. Rust, the Corresponding Secretary, presented the report of the Secretary and Treasurer, which will be found embodied in the preceding report.

Rev. Dr. Townsend, of the Boston University, was introduced, and delivered the following eloquent address:

Nearly every distinctive topic relating to the Freedmen has been presented already to the public. While reading the different annual reports of this Society, and the reports, also, of the different addresses before the several conferences; likewise while examining the reports of the American Missionary Society of the Congregational Church, and while listening to the earnest appeals from those in the South who are actively engaged in the elevation of the Freedmen, we have been struck with the recurrence of the same thoughts, and often of the same expressions; but we are likewise convinced that these repeated statements represent the more vital and fundamental thoughts which bear upon the general subject before us.

The quickened rhetorical instincts of the men who have given head and heart to this cause, and who have been thoroughly aroused to the vital interests involved, could not, in the nature of things, do otherwise than see with common eyes and speak with almost the same lips. Hence, it is not surprising that Church and State have had, already, line upon line, and precept upon precept, involving subject-matter the most solemnly truthful and the most grandly eloquent, as to our relations with the freedmen, that the human mind can conceive, or the human tongue can speak. What more need or can be said? is, therefore, a question asked by every body, as we meet in this anniversary.

We no longer need be told, for instance, that the freedmen are *men*, and that they ought to be recognized and treated as such; for this fact has been sufficiently announced, and has been perfectly demonstrated, both on the battle-field and in the school-room. We remember that the strongly prejudiced soldier of the North, seeing the heroism with which the colored troops marched to the front, and stormed the enemy's forts, lifted his cap on the field, in recognition of their manhood, and in his rough Northern accents swore that the nearly two hundred thousand freedmen, who so nobly bore the flag to victory, should never again feel the planter's lash.

In the school-room the evidence is still more convincing. The educational progress made by those black faces, under the fostering care of this Society, has compelled the acknowledgment that no children of any age or race, in view of the limited advantages heretofore enjoyed, have made, even in difficult branches, more commendable advancement.

In fact, there are so many and striking evidences of the reliable manhood and mental capacity of the freedmen in America, and of their right to equal rights, which "is the first of rights," that further argument, as to these considerations, is superfluous, and improved statement, over what has heretofore been reiterated, is next to impossible.

Often, too, and urgently, have our moral and religious obligations toward these people been argued. That the colored people have been great sufferers; that by our laws they were denied all educational privileges; that they were, in eternal equity and justice, entitled to ampler returns, and more humane treatment than they received; that those engaged in the slave traffic made the colored people heathen, and then pillaged them; and that all the principles of patriotism, philanthropy, and religion, demand restoration and restitution, are solemn and weighty matters which no conscientious soul can shake off, and which have been discussed at every anniversary of this Society since its organization. To speak upon this phase of the general subject, therefore, would be to repeat what has been spoken often, urgently, and eloquently.

The people, by this time, also, ought fully to understand the conditions and necessities which originally called the Society into existence. Repeatedly has it been stated that, when upward of four millions of slaves became freedmen, there were no specific provisions among the benevolent societies of the Church to meet these new-born wants. The Missionary Society could supply them with preachers, but they were equally in need of teachers; the Church Extension Society could aid them in building churches, but they first needed school-houses. It was to meet these conditions—to pave the way for the preacher and the Church, or rather, perhaps, to make them useful and efficient—that the Freedmen's Aid Society became a necessity. And it is a conviction among those who have examined the charities of the Church most carefully, and is shared in most fully by your speaker, that the energy and success of the organization represented here to-night, together with its magnificent opportunities for building up the kingdom of Christ, have been equaled by no benevolent enterprise of the Methodist Church. The significant recognition of its claims by the people, placing the Society, in the matter of benevolent contributions, second to no other in the Church, the present year, save the Missionary Society, must be exceedingly gratifying to its special patrons and friends. But to further enlarge upon this special topic would infringe upon the report of your Secretary.

The civil and political phases of this subject, growing out of placing the ballot in the hands of prejudice and ignorance; also, the impending perils to the Government, from collusion between defeated politicians, freedmen, and Romanists, stand among the more intensely absorbing matters involved in this subject; yet they, too, have been most solemnly argued in every city and town of the East and West. Indeed, we repeat, so thoroughly have all these vital issues been canvassed, that there really seems not only no new field to enter, but absolutely nothing new to offer from the fields already so carefully traversed. We, therefore, frankly advertise beforehand, that original material we have none; we merely group anew the great interests involved in this freedman's problem, emphasizing, however, certain matters which may be spoken with special fitness here in the National Capital.

There are two general thoughts which will be found underlying this address, and which should not, for a moment, be lost sight of. The first is, that the Almighty Father is more profoundly interested in these freedmen than is the most enthusiastic and self-sacrificing member of this Society. The second is, that there are rare opportunities in this world for rendering a given kind of service, which, if neglected, pass, and never more return. It is to this second thought we first call attention.

There are opportunities coming to men which may be called golden, others which are silvern, others brazen, others still may be termed iron, and last of all, there are opportunities which may be denominated final; they come to us attended with thunder, lightning, earthquake, and tempest. God orders that these, one after another, shall rise, pass, and be followed by their successors. There was an opportunity, taking an illustration from the field before us, golden in its features and relations, when American slavery could have been easily and handsomely removed from this country, through the personal magnanimity of leading Southern gentlemen; it was at the dawn of the Republic, when Washington, and others with him, felt keenly and deeply that the sacrifice ought to be made, seeing, as they did, that slavery and liberty were incompatible, and that slavery should end, or disaster must follow.*

There have been, likewise, other opportunities when, for instance by restrictive legislation, slavery could have been

---

* Sept., 1786, Washington wrote to Mr. John F. Mercer thus: "I never mean, unless some particular circumstance should compel me to it, to possess another slave by purchase, it being among my first wishes to see some plan adopted by which slavery in this country may be abolished by law." Eleven years afterward, he wrote to his nephew, Lawrence Lewis, thus: "I wish, from my soul, that the Legislature of this State could see the policy of a gradual abolition of slavery. It might prevent much future mischief."

quietly controlled and peacefully abolished. But, unfortunately, the system was allowed to abide, one opportunity after another passed, until nothing remained, to rid the country of it, save the earthquake and the tempest. They came; they passed; we looked about us, and saw a million of dead men, and thousands of millions of wasted money.

We speak of these matters, painful alike to North and South, only by way of illustration. In making the application of which, we grieve to say what the great laws of God's economy and providence compel us to say, namely, that the golden opportunity for making educated citizens and Protestant Christians out of the mass of the freedmen, the most desirable thing on the continent to-day, is already passed, or, at least, is rapidly passing, and when finally passed there is no power on earth to recall it. We do not say but there are favorable existing opportunities. We are unable to say just where, in this graduated scale, we to-day are, or how near we are to the era of earthquakes and tempests. We only know that we are rapidly losing what is golden, and are as rapidly approaching that which when reached shall fill the nation with dismay and anguish. These deductions are based not only upon the nature of divine providence and its historic procedures, but also upon existing tendencies, and facts so well known that none but stubborn and blind men can escape their acquaintance.

While, for illustration, the children of freedmen are still zealous in acquiring knowledge, this desire, which was once full-orbed, is fast waning with the masses of those who have passed their childhood. There was a time, during the war and shortly after, when groups of colored men in middle life, and even in life's decline, could have been seen gathered about field-stumps on which pine knots were blazing, trying thus to acquire the rudiments of an education. The enthusiasm was then at fever-heat. But this sight is at present rarely, if ever, witnessed.*

---

* Said one of the speakers at the last anniversary of Fisk University, Nashville: "At the close of the war the whole people rushed into the schools—old gray-headed men and almost helpless children. There was an impulse that carried every thing before it. Our own institution numbered at one time—1866—twelve hundred students. Then it dropped

Proper aid and encouragement have been so long withheld that the colored man is tired of waiting. Obstacles and embarrassments have stood about him so thick and seemingly insurmountable that he is already discouraged. He has also made the unfortunate discovery that ignorance does not debar from the polls, nor even from political preferment. The evening school has given way, therefore, to the political caucus. The freedmen, as would be expected, are found fast sinking into idleness and intemperance—are fast becoming tools for corrupt politicians to play with, and are falling into Roman fetichism and a worse than former licentiousness. If now any one is philosopher enough to tell how to reproduce that early blush of enthusiasm for education among the freedmen, let him speak.

Those freedmen of the West Indies will not easily return to the condition of mind which was theirs when they passed the threshold of slavery; so also of the freedmen of the United States. "The dawn comes twice to no man," says an ancient African proverb. As it appears to us, second-rate opportunities, at best those beset with increasing embarrassments and discouragements, now remain to those engaged in the educational elevation of that people. True as inspiration is Shakspeare's text:

> "There is a tide in the affairs of men,
> Which, taken at the flood, leads on to fortune;
> Omitted, all the voyage of their life
> Is bound in shallows and in miseries."

---

down to less than three hundred." There are ample data upon which to establish on general grounds these deductions. We need, perhaps, refer to but a single instance, inasmuch as it is one that furnishes an illustration which is almost an exact parallel to the case before us. When the blacks of the British West Indies were emancipated they manifested a zeal for education only second to that shown by the freedmen of America; but to-day, especially in Jamaica, "the liberated slaves," says Colonel Baylor, "have relapsed into degrading sloth, if not also into barbarism." No one who has investigated this case questions but it might have been otherwise. The fatal mistakes were in diminishing their wages to such a pittance as required all their energies to eke out a mere subsistence; also the withdrawal of all government aid by way of educational provisions; likewise, the absence of personal encouragement to people so much needing it, and without which the emancipated will seldom if ever do otherwise than lapse gradually from their first ambitions and aims into idleness and indifference.

Heine felicitously remarked that "every age is a sphinx, which sinks into the earth as soon as its problem is solved." We may add, never to rise save in some other form.

What has been said as to elevating the freedmen into educated citizens applies also as to making of them consistent Protestant Christians. No one can fail to see that Christian effort is met already with increasing and embarrassing difficulties. Little did the colored people know, ten years since, as to infidelity. To-day they are successfully taught to part with Christ by men who carry them a loaf of bread. They have accepted the loaf, and the mind has been poisoned with doubt. Though, in justice to their native instincts, it ought to be said, as yet the number of such is limited.

Ten years ago the Romanist bore no love for the slave, but since he has become a freedman, and since the ballot has been placed in his hand, he has been visited by all branches of Roman Catholic charities; he has been embraced by the priest and received into his fold. The eyes of many of these ignorant and superstitious colored people have been strongly allured toward Romish pomp, show, and ceremony; they have already devoutly kissed the crucifix. Could they be expected to do otherwise? Not only this, but the freedman has discovered that he is less troubled by his enemy when becoming a Romanist, and more so if he becomes a Methodist. He has also learned that his body is better provided for when he makes the sign of the cross; is it a matter of wonder if he asks, Why shall I not make it?

In the hour of sickness the Sister of Charity comes to his relief, while the Methodist sister does not or can not cross his threshold; is it a matter of surprise that he has welcomed such as an angel of mercy?

Those of the freedmen who still desire education for themselves or their children, seeing that Protestants are hesitating and closing their schools even while filled with pupils, and seeing Romanists opening new schools in every quarter, have asked, Why may we not form these new and apparently permanent and beneficial alliances?

The reasons as yet assigned for not doing this have neither convinced nor prevented them. The Boston secretary of the American Missionary Society has remarked recently that, in certain localities, being obliged to discontinue their schools for lack of funds, the colored children *en masse* had gone into the neighboring Catholic schools, which were eagerly opened to receive them. And, worse than all else for Protestantism, this course has been strongly advocated by the leading negroes of the North. George T. Downing, an educated and intelligent colored man, has been so nettled with the disabilities and abuses of his people, and with the caste and prejudices of Protestant Churches against them, that he declares the Catholic Church to be the only reliable refuge of freedmen.

"All that the poor downtrodden blacks of the United States have to do," he says, "is to 'fellowship' with this strong, courageous, well-disciplined Church, and they thereby become, not only a part of her power, but add to the power which will protect them."

He further says: "I am fully persuaded that a general alliance, on the part of the colored people of America, with the Catholic Church of America, would be the most speedy and effective agency to break down American caste, based on color."

The colored people are not slow to discover these apparent advantages, especially when approved and urged by the educated of their own nationality. As might be expected, by public resolutions they have recognized this deep interest of Romanism in their educational welfare, and have formally conferred with the authorities of the Catholic Church to ascertain to what extent they may look to it for assistance. Under the circumstances, who has the heart to condemn them?*

---

* The American Missionary Association erected, in Macon, Ga., a large and commodious school building, and for several years maintained a flourishing school in it. For the last two years, an arrangement has been effected by which the county school board rents the building and pays the salaries of the teachers, who are appointed by the Association, which thus secures good Northern teachers for the colored people, saves the expense of their salaries, and, at the same time, shows a readiness to co-operate with the South in educational efforts.

Recently, the school board of the county decided to discontinue the arrangement, declined to employ our teachers, and assigned the hottest months in the year for the colored schools. A meeting of the colored people of Macon was held, June 27th, in which the action of the board was recited and censured, and resolutions adopted looking toward relief. We

But, replies some one, suppose the Papist does assume the education of the colored people, what objection is there? At this point we are not dealing with objections to such movements. As yet we have not said that there are objections. We are simply establishing facts—the fact that Protestantism has been slow to see her most favorable opportunity, and backward in availing herself of it; also, the fact that Romanism has been quick to recognize hers, and ready, quietly, steadily, and persistently, to embrace and render it available; the fact that the funds of the Protestant Church are at present withheld, and her schools in the South closed, in part, perhaps, because her business men at the North are paralyzed, every other one of whom, to speak with exaggeration, is a bankrupt; also, the fact that Romanists, with seemingly ample wealth, are multiplying their schools, and are pressing steadily and surely on to the vantage-ground; the fact that Protestants, not having broken down their caste prejudices, are slowly but surely alienating their natural friends; also, the fact that the Jesuit, always the shrewd and artful, but respectful and condescending, servant of the Church, willing to become "not merely the equal, but the inferior, of the lowest," by boasting that he sees no difference between souls on account of the color of the skin, and by looking carefully after all forms of distress and want, is

---

copy a portion of the resolutions, as published in the *Macon Telegraph and Messenger* of June 28th:

"*Resolved*, That we appoint a committee for the purpose of corresponding with Rev. Mr. Strieby, Secretary of the American Missionary Association, for the purpose of obtaining the assistance of that organization in our effort to continue the Lewis High-school; also,

"*Whereas*, the Catholic Church has recently given so many manifestations indicative of a deep interest in the educational welfare of the colored people; and, *whereas*, the recent action of the school board of this county, in changing the scholastic year, in discontinuing our most flourishing school, and in dispensing with the services of our most efficient and experienced teachers, will undoubtedly force us to look for assistance in the educational work from other sources than those on which we have heretofore depended;

"*Resolved*, That this meeting appoint a committee to wait upon Right Rev. Bishop Gross, who is now in the city, to obtain his views as to the educational policy of the Catholic Church in regard to the colored people of the South, and to ascertain to what extent we may look to that organization for assistance in the work of educating our children."

conquering that colored population, and strongly alluring it to the arch-enemy of the Protestant faith.*

We repeat, our effort has not been, thus far, to say why these conditions ought not to exist, but simply to show that they do exist; and, in view of their existence, that we are compelled to confess that the golden opportunity, the one freest from embarrassment, in efforts to save the colored population of the South to the Protestant Christian faith, and therefore the opportunity of binding them firmly to Christ and the republic, *is already passed*. We dislike to be forced to these conclusions; it is exceedingly annoying, publicly, to announce them, but to suppress the truth may be worse, in the end, than to be frank and above-board in our admissions. Such are the leading considerations which induce us, in this address, to plead thrice:

First. With the Protestant Church.
Second. With the General Government.
Third. With the white people of the Southern States.

It would be desirable, if, *in the plea to the Church*, time were allowed to paint the splendid era for general Christian enterprise through which this age is passing, and especially to

---

* The following address of Archbishop Manning, at the consecration of certain missionaries sent to the Southern field, may be interesting: "These priests go as the van-guard of others who will soon follow, inflamed with the love of souls; souls not lovable for their intelligence and virtue, but souls black with ignorance and vice; lovable only because your Master died for them. You give yourselves forever to be the fathers and servants of the negroes, and to labor exclusively for them until your death, in the spirit of Peter Clavor, who announced himself as forever the slave of the slave."

Each of the missionaries kneeled down, and holding in his hand an open Bible, took this vow of consecration upon himself. The venerable Archbishop then arose, prostrated himself before each missionary, embraced his feet, and then, arising, kissed each upon both cheeks, receiving a similar kiss in return.

The following item is taken from a recent issue of the *Montgomery* (Ala.) *Advertiser:* "The Catholic Church is making a determined effort to extend their educational work in the South. The headquarters of this effort are in Baltimore, where the priests, nuns, and sisters from abroad report, and are detailed to various parts of the South. New schools for colored children are to be immediately opened, as follows: ten in Georgia, fifteen in Alabama, fifteen in Mississippi, and twenty-five in Louisiana. These schools will offer board and tuition free to colored young men and women."

point out the magnificent part it is the almost exclusive privilege of this country to enact. Our limits, however, permit only the briefest indication of these important matters and relations.

The races, starting from Central Asia, traveling East and West, reached at length the European Atlantic and the Asiatic Pacific coasts, and at those boundaries seemed providentially held in check for centuries.

At a time when occasions had ripened into fullness, this New World, so long within, yet beyond, the grasp of nations was discovered, to which, ever since, though limited through the earlier years of its occupancy by Europeans, have all peoples and tongues been tending. No nationality is to-day without its representatives. Of those having come, some have remained; but others, filled with new ideas, have returned to their native lands. The exclusive Chinaman is now seeking American citizenship, and is passing freely between this land and his own vast empire. Many of these Mongolians are comprehending the advantages of our civilization, and hundreds are christianized, and then, quickly filled with longings to return to their native country to christianize their kindred, become faithful evangelists. What is true of Chinamen is equally true of other peoples. In fine, America is now to the nations of the earth what Jerusalem was to the Roman Empire on the day of Pentecost. That day, in more than one respect, is typical of the day in which we live. Jerusalem was, at that time, the home "of men out of every nation" under heaven: "Parthians, and Medes, and Elamites, and the dwellers in Mesopotamia, and in Judea, and Cappadocia, in Pontus, and Asia, Phrygia, and Pamphylia, in Egypt, and in the parts of Libya about Cyrene, and strangers of Rome, Jews and proselytes, Cretes and Arabians." This, also, and more, can be said of America.

The English tongue, like the Greek during the Roman ascendency, is universal. Missionaries are beginning to declare the Gospel of Christ in English speech in China, in India, in some of the islands of the sea, and elsewhere; and, as if by miracle, every man is hearing "the wonderful works of God" as if spoken in his own tongue, or, at least, is comprehending the thought spoken better than when expressed in the crude speech of an imperfect master of a tongue, as most missionaries must, of necessity, be.*

Chinamen, with many others, are at present laying aside Bibles translated into their own language, and are reading, with marked success, the common English version.†

Not only this, but our position and our tongue have achieved the grand conquest in moral and spiritual power vainly desired by Archimedes in physics, and, without stepping

---

* It would, probably, have been wiser from the start, for missionaries never to have attempted, at least in certain countries, to instruct in other than English speech. Many languages are destitute of the symbols with which to express Christian ideas. Christian termonology depends, in considerable measure, upon previous Christian thinking and living. This principle should certainly govern present missionary work, since all people are eager to understand the conquering tongue of the world—the English.

† We call especial attention to the Chinese, because they are already represented in the United States by more than a hundred thousand of their people, who, with the Africans, represent half the population of the globe.

There is a forcible putting of this special subject in a recent circular by Mr. Woodworth, of the American Missionary Society: "China is substantially as heathen and unsaved as she was 1800 years ago, though no people in the world have been more persistently plied with missionary agencies. It is not unlikely that one of the apostles wandered as far East as China, and there preached the Gospel. At any rate, the Nestorian missionaries were there in force from the fifth to the twelfth centuries; the Portuguese, the Spanish, and the Italian missionaries, from that time to the sixteenth century; and the Dutch, from the latter date until now. English missionaries were there as early as 1807, and the Americans in 1829, and still China is grim, dark, and defiant as of old.

"After having tried, for eighteen centuries, on those lines, to take China for Christ, and *failed*, is it not worth considering whether there may not be another line of attack? Is it not possible that we are to win success for China by the way of the Pacific slopes? One needs to reflect only a moment to see what an immense advantage we have in our mission schools in California to prepare the best missionaries for China. Confessedly, no foreign missionary can preach in a strange tongue as a native can, nor wield such influence among his people. Will it not be something worse than a blunder, then, if we do not take advantage of the thousands who are among us, for the Chinese empire?

"The eagerness of the colored people for the labors of teachers and missionaries is the marvel of the age, but it is only exceeded by the eagerness of the Chinese to learn the English language, and to read the English Bible. Within the last six months, thirty-nine have professed conversion in connection with our mission schools in California, a number equal to the fruits of the previous three years, showing how rapidly the work is deepening and widening."

from our shores, we hold in our hands the lever, and occupy a position such as enables us easily to move and elevate the whole world.

Now, it would seem that no one, who has given any thought to this subject, can fail to see the important, nay, the mighty part, to be achieved by the freedmen of America, in these movements to elevate and save the nations of the earth, our country henceforth being the grand center of influence and power.

These African race-lines, extending into the West India Islands, on into South America, and over the entire continent of Africa, awaken the deepest interest in every contemplative mind, for the finger of God seems directing these American ex-slaves, in harmony with his sublime methods of procedure, to go with the Gospel to the one hundred and eighty millions of their scattered race.

Heretofore the salvation of Africa has been the most difficult problem in missionary calculation and effort. During the last century and a half there have been noble and heroic attempts to christianize that continent, but failure after failure, with the apparently fruitless sacrifice of scores of true and devoted men, have been the painful results.[*]

But if we mistake not, this difficult problem is in process of self-solution. Africa is to be redeemed by her own sons. Ten thousand scholars are now under training in the Southern States for this ultimate object. Christian people who have contributed to this Society have thought they were merely aiding in relieving the physical wants of an unfortunate people. Grander than this is God's design; he is planning that these thousands of young men and women who are at school in this republic, breathing more and more the atmosphere of its Christian civilization, recognizing more and more their ordained mission, shall at length receive the spirit of his inspiration, and go forth "by twos" and by hundreds,

---

[*] The history of the disastrous attempt to carry the Gospel to Africa in 1841, also in 1861, under the patronage of the British Government, with every appliance that wealth, learning, and piety could provide, should be carefully studied in these times, when a reconstruction of missionary movements and efforts seems inevitable.

with the grandest attempts and, prospectively, the grandest achievements in the history of Christian evangelization.*

I wish I could reach the ear of every colored man in the South. I would say to him, "O brother, God now designs that you shall save your race!" I would tell him that all history proves that the regenerator of a people must ultimately arise from the people regenerated. Moses was not an Egyptian, but an Israelite; Confucius was not a Chaldean, but a Chinaman; Zoroaster was not an Assyrian, but a Persian; Sakya Muni was not a Babylonian, but a Hindoo; so also Mahommed was an Arabian, Luther a German, Wesley an Englishman, and the Lord Jesus was a *man*, though God. No angel nor archangel could have wrought the regeneration of the human race. The law is universal.

Let every teacher under the direction of this Society be consistently urged to press the thought of their ordained self-redemption upon the minds of these colored people. Let the idea be repeated and emphasized until at length, like a burden, it shall rest upon their minds and hearts; anon, some of their number will grasp the idea in its fullness, and when they do, and as fast as they do, they will no longer remain the groveling race they now are, but will be seized with an inspiration such as will ennoble and elevate them far beyond any possibilities we have conceived respecting them. Such, it seems to us, is God's pleasure. But, as already intimated, he has conditioned the accomplishment of these ends upon

---

*The ripe condition of Africa for such enterprises may be inferred from information recently given us by Mr. Stanley. We take the following from the London *Spectator*: "Mr. Stanley has revisited, in Central Africa, King Mtesa, ruler of Uganda, who was formerly a mere savage but who has embraced Mohammedanism, and organized his kingdom, which covers five great tracts, upon a semi-civilized basis. In the course of conversation, Mr. Stanley convinced Mtesa that Mohammedanism was erroneous, and the king now asks for a Christian mission to instruct him and his subjects. The story, with the sudden conversion of King Mtesa in a few hours' talk, carried on through an interpreter, reads very oddly; but Mr. Stanley clearly believes it himself, and his demand has been at once complied with. A gentleman has promised ten thousand pounds to the Church Missionary Society, if they will take advantage of the opportunity thus opened, and the munificent offer has, pending further discussion, been accepted."

the faithful co-operation of the Christian Church. There can be no question that the Church is called to aid in preparing this people to comprehend an idea which, as yet, owing to their years of servitude and degeneration, is above their reach.

Before this African Moses shall arise, he *must be taken into the king's family*, and be taught as was that Jewish law-giver, in all the arts and sciences of the land in which he had been a bondman.

Before this African Confucius shall arise, he must be taught until he embodies in himself the moral and civil codes of the land of his adoption, and until he is the representation of our national wisdom, whose words, reduced to maxims and laws, shall hold sway over the millions of his people as he helps them on from barbarism to Christian civilization.

Before this African Luther shall arise, he must be a certified master in the most distinguished universities of the republic, and must also be aided in planting his feet upon the fundamental doctrine of the Christian Church—justification by faith alone.

Before this African John Wesley shall arise, he must be able to stand with the leading scholars of the land of his birth, and must be of that " company of men having the form and seeking the power of godliness."

Indeed, can any thing be clearer than this, that it is the imperative and inevitable duty of the Christian Church to hasten its aid in laying these broad and liberal foundations for the redemption of the African people at the hands of these whom Providence has placed at our doors? Must not the Church sow the divine seed which is to elevate and christianize the freedmen, and through them their kindred in the West India Islands, in South America, and throughout the African continent?

With such possibilities actualizing while we contemplate them; with such direct and indirect opportunities opening and closing their doors while we stand before them; with the calls of Providence sounding in our ears with a majesty never before surpassed, even if equaled, and with this rare privilege of evoking from these colored masses their regenerator, is not the indolence and indifference of the Church of Christ astounding? God would have this incomprehensively sublime work done, and Christian people are hesitating; they who are by divine appointment and by divine ordination the salt of the earth and the light of the world, the servants to gather in the destitute to the feast, and the branches which must bear the fruit of the Christ-vine, are more than half asleep. With such opportunities unimproved, with such a mission, commanded by Jehovah, yet unfulfilled, is it a matter of wonder that our costly and elegant houses of worship in the North seemed cursed of heaven, in which religion lies before the altar voiceless and dead?

We do not hesitate to say that the apathy of certain Methodist Churches respecting this Southern work is one of the most startling evidences of either a fatal blindness to properly apprehend the sublime issues pending, or else of a coldness indicating that the Spirit of Christ no longer burns upon their altars.*

But some one replies, You discourage us. You confess that the golden opportunity has passed; what remains is second-rate, and we prefer to do nothing. We felt sure some

---

* The plea for help coming to this Society from those in the field is pitiful. The following from one of our teachers is representative: "Your Society must aid us, or we shall be compelled to give up our work and return North. With the aid of one hundred dollars we can keep up our school and Church, and do a great work for Christ. Christ must have some one who loves him and has the means, and who will keep us from *starvation* while we preach to and teach this poor people. My heart is almost broken as I contemplate the desolation around me, and the indifference that prevails in the Church in reference to this Southern work."

But, notwithstanding, only about one-half of the Methodist Churches of the land have taken the appointed collection for this cause the past year.

The last reports of the American Missionary Society likewise implore the Churches for funds; but the Churches do not respond. Said the Boston secretary the other day, Many of our preachers decline to have the cause presented to their people. Dr. Kirk said to us, just before his death, that the Congregationalist pastors blocked the progress of this Southern missionary movement, and offer all manner of frivolous excuses when asked to have the cause presented to their people.

The scholars who have graduated from the schools under the management of that Society, and who are fully prepared to teach, and who have desired to consecrate themselves to this service, have been waiting to be set to work, but "hope deferred," says the report, "has driven many from their high purposes into secular employments, or, worse, into a shiftless and discouraged idleness."

one would say that. But it is only a wretched excuse of professional excuse-makers.

When the better opportunities for defending Athens against the aggressions of Philip had passed, and when Demosthenes was blamed for persisting in a lost cause, and for embracing the next best course, he nobly replied: "Had we resigned without a struggle that which our ancestors encountered every danger to win, who would not have spit upon us?" Let our wavering Christian faith receive rebuke from that pagan orator.

> "They never fail who die
> In a great cause,"

should be the repeated watchword along the Christian ranks. Indeed, with failures, as Christians, we have nothing to do, save to regret such past failures as have resulted from our own unfaithfulness.

Christian enterprise is never to cease, if the results are always disastrous. Our Lord commended the poor widow who cast her money in the public treasury, though the commonwealth was cursed. And he himself trod his weary way to Calvary, though he knew every step led him to a cross. Christian courage requires us to go into battle, not merely when we are sure of victory, but when we are equally sure of defeat.

But this representation is too desperate. All is not lost. Though the better occasion is past, the present is pressing, grand and sublime enough to enlist importunate prayers from every Christian heart, liberal gifts from every Christian Church, and personal sacrifice from every disciple of our Lord throughout the land.

The present opportunity, such as it is, is ours; what will be to-morrow, we can not tell; we only know that if the present is unimproved, to-morrow's opportunity, in its relation to us, will be beset with augmented embarrassments, while the Church, as if under a divine judgment, shall be more and more crippled, and less and less able to cope with that which but lately could have been easily accomplished.*

---

* We may perhaps infer the Divine interest in these colored people, likewise the expression of Divine displeasure at the indifference of his Church,

Keeping in mind the fundamental principles thus far governing this discussion—vanishing opportunities, and the ever-watchful and interested eye of God—*we offer our second plea, directed to the National Government.* We anticipate so far as to say that this part of the address involves a petition to Congress to aid the educational societies already in the field, whose especial object is to educate and christianize the Freedmen.

The affirmation needs no qualification, that the importance of such aid can be equaled by no measure that is to be presented to the approaching Congress. This thought may be examined, somewhat critically, for a moment. It is no trifling affair, as every body knows, to place that bit of white paper, with a name upon it, called a ballot, between the thumb and finger of an American citizen. Repeated, in all our households, should be the startling counsels of one who saw most clearly the force of this consideration:

"The human imagination can picture no semblance of the destructive potency of the ballot-box in the hands of an ignorant and corrupt people. The Roman cohorts were terrible; the Turkish janizaries were incarnate fiends: but each

---

from certain prophetic announcements. Haggai spoke of the Jewish temple. But humanity is now God's temple. (1 Cor. iii, 16.) We may therefore substitute, for temple, colored people. The passage will then read: "Thus speaketh the Lord of hosts, saying, This people say, The time is not come, the time that the Lord's *colored people* should be built up. Then came the word of the Lord by Haggai, the prophet, saying, Is it time for you, O ye, to dwell in your ceiled houses, and this *colored people* lie waste? Now therefore thus saith the Lord of hosts: Consider your ways. Ye have sown much, and bring in little; ye eat, but ye have not enough; ye drink, but ye are not filled with drink; ye clothe you, but there is none warm; and he that earneth wages, earneth wages to put it into a bag with holes. Thus saith the Lord of hosts: Consider your ways. Ye looked for much, and, lo, it came to little; and when ye brought it home, I did blow upon it. Why? saith the Lord of hosts. Because of my *people* that is waste, and ye run every man unto his own house." (Haggai i, 2-9.)

It is not difficult to see that as a nation we are now passing through identically such experiences. But our continued indifference will result still more disastrously. It shall soon be said: "Therefore the heaven over you is stayed from dew, and the earth is stayed from her fruit. And I called for a drought upon the land, and upon the mountains, and upon the corn, and upon the new wine, and upon the oil, and upon that which the ground bringeth forth, and upon men, and upon cattle, and upon all the labor of the hands." (Haggai i, 10, 11.)

was powerless as a child for harm, compared with universal suffrage without mental illumination and moral principle. The power of casting a vote is far more formidable than that of casting spear or javelin. On one of those oft-recurring days, when the fate of the State or the Union is to be decided at the polls; when, all over the land, the votes are falling as thick as hail, and we seem to hear them rattle like the clangor of arms, it is enough to make the lover of his country turn pale to reflect upon the motives under which they may be given, and the consequences to which they may lead."

It is, indeed, a fearful condition, when ignorance and a blind selfishness may wield the same power, man for man, as is vested in the wisdom and patriotism of the most enlightened. Nay, more. We firmly believe, that, if the millions of this country, who are "clothed with the royal right of suffrage, and who are holding in their hands the sovereign power of this nation," are not suitably educated for the trusts committed to them, it is only a question of time when American republicanism shall be betrayed, and then terminate in anarchy and monarchy.*

---

* It is not difficult to establish this position upon historic data, which present parallels startlingly significant. They were ignorant and deluded masses, who demanded a king, in the time of Samuel, in place of the essentially republican commonwealth under which they might have been blessed. (1 Sam. viii.) Athens might have remained a grand republic until the present, had the majorities of her people been properly educated; but, lacking this, the political condition of Athens was fickle beyond endurance. Her best men were exiled or put to death, while the unscrupulous were raised to the head of the State. At length, annoyed by such disasters as are likely to overtake any people without culture and intelligence enough to comprehend the results of their folly, they, with other Greeks, allowed internal dissensions to work such weakness and discouragement, that Athens fell an easy prey to Roman conquest. Rome, too, after she became a pure democracy, could have remained thus, had her citizens received proper education. The ignorant masses, the lower orders of whom were despicable, were dazzled with the phantom of military glory, as the Israelites had been, and submitted to violating the constitution, by prolonging the term of office in the case of successful chieftains, so that the consul of a year became dictator for life. The next step was easy—that of perpetual and hereditary emperorship—and the republican constitution of Rome became a thing of history; and that step, in this country, unless the masses are educated, will be more easily and far sooner taken than we of to-day imagine.

It must be confessed that our legislation in these matters has been blind, if not reckless. The contingencies incident to well-nigh unrestricted suffrage and unlimited immigration, are actually appalling. Before this recent deluge of the races had begun to set in upon the United States, they ought to have been more thoroughly rooted in their hundred years of history, and have had such protective legislation as would shield from impending dangers. Emerson has a significant remark: "Formerly, we imported foreign goods; we now import foreign workmen, and manufacture the goods. Which is the wiser course, remains to be seen." Well may we ponder the problem. Looking at our condition, as it to-day presents itself, and seeing that the nation is imperiled through past political blunders, can Congress do less, as a national safeguard, than to provide for the most speedy moral and educational development possible, in case of all those who cast the vote; and whenever, of its own accord, any State of the Union does not thus provide, ought it not to be compelled by the general government, on the grounds of political foresight and safety, to make such provision? But, if a given State of the Union, through misfortunes or disasters of any kind, is unable to do this, then ought not the general government itself to make such provisions? At all events, and by some means, ought not this doctrine to be at once and forever established: The voting citizens of America shall not be allowed to remain illiterate.*

But to be more specific. Up to the close of the civil war, there was no true free-school system in any Southern State. Indeed, the laws of the Slave States positively forbade the majority of her people from learning even the rudiments of education. The slaves were freed; those lawless laws, which imposed perpetual ignorance, were abrogated; the Freedmen's

---

* George Washington clearly saw, in his day, the importance of common intelligence in a republic, and regarded provisions "for the general diffusion of knowledge as of primary importance." "There is not a power vested by the Constitution, either in the Congress or the people," says Judge Hoar, "toward the exercise and accomplishment of which the education of the people is not the surest, the most direct, and the cheapest way." Mr. Gladstone, with a keen eye to national interests, has declared that the "victory of Germany over France is the victory of the common-school system of Prussia over the ignorance of the French empire."

Bureau was established, and it did a grand, independent work, and also gave valuable assistance to this, and likewise to other societies engaged in this Southern work: but, after rendering this valuable service for a few years, the Government, owing to one reason and another, was induced to discontinue the Bureau, and has now practically forsaken her ignorant, but liberated and enfranchised people. This can not be looked upon, politically, in any other light than as one of the most fearful mistakes ever made by any government on earth, existing or historic. But inspect these matters still more closely. Thirty-nine per cent of the voters in the Southern States are to-day unable to read. Think of the ballot held in the hands of 1,157,000 men who can not read! And, what is worse, there are no enforced measures to make it otherwise—this, too, in a country where "there are two things that can reach the top of the pyramid," as D'Alembert says, "the eagle and the reptile."

Now, we will presume that the destitution at the South is such that liberal measures in educational matters can not be provided. Repeated losses, heavy taxations, frequent foreclosures, wild disturbances, and prostrated industries, are resting with distressing weight upon those Southern States.

We may safely say that it is, practically, impossible for the few people in the South who have property to supply means for educating these eleven or twelve millions of citizens, including blacks and whites, who can not be denied the humanizing and ennobling influences of learning and religion without imminent peril to our national existence.*

But we repeat, if these States, in their poverty and desolation, can not do otherwise, that is, if they can not properly

---

* We are not surprised at the late report of the Commissioner of Education, that, in North Carolina, the yearly expenditure for every child between six and sixteen years of age is but .62; that in Alabama a large number of the free-schools in the country districts have been closed, owing to the impoverished condition of the people; that, in Arkansas, teachers, unable to secure their salaries, in many instances, have abandoned their schools and quit the State. We need not be surprised that the case is no better in Louisiana, while, by certain changes in the school-laws of Texas, the educational system of that State has an existence only in name. Such, unfortunately, are the facts; and, at present, we are not sure that these States can do otherwise.

provide for the education of the people, then, by all the claims and dictates of political safety, the Government itself must make the provision. How shall this be done, is, perhaps, a difficult matter to decide. It may be difficult to reestablish the Freedman's Bureau; it may be difficult to build up a school system exclusively under national patronage; but what objection can be urged should the Government generously aid the schools already established, and respecting whose thorough work and discipline there is no question? Other parties will officially represent their own Church enterprises South. We may speak a word for the Freedmen's Aid Society.*

This Society has already aided fifty thousand colored people to acquire an education. More than a thousand are now in preparation, whose special object is, to elevate their race by teaching and preaching. This Society is providing schools of a high order in Maryland, Virginia, North Carolina, South Carolina, in Florida, two in Georgia, one in Alabama, one in Mississippi, three in Louisiana, one in Tennessee, and one in Texas.

This Society has acquired and built up in the Southern States a school property worth to-day $200,000. We ask again, if the South is too poor to make educational provision for her people, or if the general government can not, or will not, enforce educational measures in those States, why will it not aid these societies, which are obliged, at the present time, from a lack of means, to retrench their work, closing their doors against thousands of children who would gladly enter them?†

---

* Prominent among these enterprises are the societies under the patronage of the Congregational, Baptist, Presbyterian, and Episcopalian Churches. Among the foremost stands the American Missionary Association. This Association has ample accommodations in the South for twenty thousand pupils though, for lack of funds, half this number are debarred from these privileges. Their report says that their arrangements are such that, in most of their schools, the sum of seventy dollars, in addition to what a student can earn by work out of school hours, by teaching in vacation and in other ways, will enable him to clothe himself and attend school during the year.

† It is possible that some one will object, upon the ground that, in these denominational schools, moral and religious as well as intellectual train-

Let us not be misunderstood in making these statements. The design is not to shirk any tasks belonging properly to the Church. We would prefer to have the Government itself attend to the general education of her people. When this is done, we would spurn, rather than ask, aid. Nay, more: if the Government will faithfully enter upon this work of education, the Church will gladly abandon the Freedmen's Aid Society, and henceforth apply itself to purely missionary work. Still, we are willing to remain; we are willing to send our teachers South; we are willing to aid in infusing intelligence into the ballot, that demagogism and priestcraft may be shorn of their might; but what we ask, and in all reason justly ask, is that Congress, in this our extremity, will put forth its hand to protect and aid. Perhaps it is not becoming in us to advance a step further, and offer a warning as well as an entreaty. But it is clear to every body that *something* must be done by the Government, or, as true as there is a God in heaven, there is to be another national earthquake.

ing are attended to. Well, suppose that is the case, will any one object who has the nation's weal at heart, or who realizes that the object of an education is to perfect the individual?

It should be settled that education can not be complete if the moral faculties are not developed. The Prussians have a maxim, that "whatever you would have appear in a nation's life, you must put into the public-schools."

European nations, who have borrowed from us the common-school system, have, in certain respects, gone in advance of us, by showing that "the idea of educating a moral being, while wholly ignoring and excluding moral influences, is preposterous." We may do worse than to learn a lesson from modern atheists and materialists. Huxley, one of the most noted English advocates of a form of materialism which practically excludes God from the universe, has recently pronounced very decidedly in favor of the introduction of the Bible as a *reading book* into common-schools. His position is, that "there must be a moral substratum to a child's education to make it valuable; and that there is no other source from which this can be obtained at all comparable with the Bible."

Says Chief-Justice Shaw: "The public-school system was intended to provide a system of moral training. Hence, the removal of the Bible gives us an incomplete basis of education, and defeats the intention of the public-school system."

Andrew Jackson, during his last illness, pointed a friend to the Bible, remarking, "That book, sir, is the rock upon which our republic rests."

"If we abide by its principles," said Daniel Webster, "our country will go on prospering and to prosper; but if we and our posterity neglect

Congress has been trying to reconstruct the South these ten years, more or less, but with no very brilliant success. The prospects, at this very hour, are as gloomy as midnight. Significant were the prophetic and almost last words of Mr. Wilson, that the next conflict in this country is to be on the question of union and disunion. But why have not these matters been already adjusted? What is the difficulty? This: Never can there be order and peace in those States while remaining in their present dense illiteracy. Legislation here in Washington will continue to amount to nothing; the Southern States will remain irritable and fretted; the whites will

---

its instruction and *authority*, no man can tell how sudden a catastrophe may overwhelm us, and bury all our glory in profound obscurity."

"So great is my veneration for the Bible," said John Quincy Adams, "that the earlier my children begin to read it, the more confident will be my hopes that they will prove useful citizens to their country, and respectable members of society."

These are a few of the many confessions of the eminent and liberal-minded men of our country, respecting the importance of Biblical truth in our national government and culture. The safety of teaching the moral and spiritual truths of the Protestant Bible and the Protestant religion in our public-schools may be argued also upon the ground of their beneficial influence throughout the world. The morality of civilized nations is not based upon Confucius, Zoroaster, Buddha, or Church Councils, but upon the Protestant Bible. In fact, upon whatever portion of the earth the eye falls, it discovers high civilization, general intelligence, and national prosperity, just in proportion to the prevalence of Biblical truth and the Protestant faith.

But granting these principles, it may be still further objected: If the Government extends its aid to the Protestant educational societies in the South, it can not escape extending its aid to Roman Catholic schools. In the first place, a distinction could, with propriety, be made in favor of Protestant schools, on the ground that our political institutions were originally founded, not upon Judaism, Mormonism, nor upon Roman Catholicism, but upon Protestantism. They could not possibly have originated in either of the other named systems. Our Declaration of Independence, our National and State Constitutions, are imbued with Protestantism. They are a protest against all kinds of usurpation and intolerance. Indeed, the very genius of American Republicanism is Protestantism. These are not matters of controversy, but simple facts. There can, therefore, be no impropriety in extending special favors to those principles upon which this republic was founded. We must faithfully protect the general interests of all sects, including Jews, Chinese, and Roman Catholics, as citizens, but we can not hazard their personal liberty as well as ours by disowning the mother who bore us. The debt this nation owes to Protestantism forbids

remain angry and embittered, either sullenly standing aloof from politics, or else carrying nothing but passion and violence into political contests; intimidation, outrage, and assassination will be augmented; the industries will be more and more crippled; life and property will be more and more insecure; contempt, bitterness, and hate will be more and more intensified,—unless there shall be radical changes in the methods of legislative procedures. Despite all attempted reconstruction, those States are in a worse condition to-day than the day the war closed, and under the same policy of

---

that any other system or creed should stand for a moment in competition with it.

But, in the second place, that Roman Catholic schools should not only not receive aid, but should be suppressed, must be clear to every considerate mind. Romanism seeks to make civil authority amenable to ecclesiastical supremacy; therefore, no consistent Roman Catholic has a right to call himself an American citizen. His sworn allegiance is not to State authority, but to the Pope of Rome. We cheerfully and gratefully acknowledge that many anti-Protestant patriots fought and bled in our late civil struggle, also in our earlier Revolution, and that the names of Roman Catholics have an honorable place on our Declaration of Independence. But the normal tendencies of popery will eventuate in the subversion of political freedom, and, therefore, should be shown no patronage by the Government; and when its ideas are disseminated, they deserve prosecution on the ground of treason.

The conclusions are: First, in a republic, the Government must reserve the right to superintend the education of the children, for upon their correct education depends the perpetuity of constitutional liberty. In a republic, there must be school-houses for children, or there will have to be barracks for soldiers. Common-school education, therefore, is not simply a privilege, but is, in our country, a public necessity. If, to teach a boy to read and write, has a tendency to make him a better citizen, it becomes the duty of the State to compel him to attend school for that purpose.

Second, the moral and religious nature of the child can no more be neglected in its education than can the intellectual. Indeed, intellectual training, independent of the moral, may result in the conversion of an ordinary, into an extraordinary, villain.

Third, Government, upon the principle of self-preservation, must also object to the establishment of any school, and the expenditure of any public moneys in the interests of any system of education, or in the interests of any religious sect, which disseminates ideas opposed to free institutions and democratic principles. That is, the Government should not allow any ideas to be publicly indorsed and promulgated which are anti-republican, and which do not recognize in the *State*, instead of in an *Ecclesiastic*, the highest embodiment of civil authority.

Congress will be worse to-morrow, and still worse the day following..

The truth is, our Congress has been adding to the disturbance of the waters that overflow, while the trouble is with the fountain, which has not been touched. Congress has been trying to repair the superstructure, while the foundations are mire and quicksand. It has been trying to reconstruct the man, leaving the child in pollution. Our "political economy never studies prevention," it never cleanses the sewers, it only curses the fever-stricken. Congress must go deeper than it has yet gone in the work of reconstruction, even before any perceptible advance is made. The alternative is: liberal educational measures, or illiterate States, North or South, placed under territorial rule, one or the other; but the outcry against the invasion of State rights, even if the Government seeks to quell State disturbances, forbids the latter measure. Our Executive is, unfortunately, trammeled. But the other course—the provision of liberal educational measures—can be adopted. Why is it not? It is now generally acknowledged, as it was frequently remarked during the war, that it was the prevailing ignorance of the Southern white people which rendered it possible for a few skilled leaders to take the seceding States out of the Union, and into rebellion and war. And yet, incredible as it may seem, the national Government is doing comparatively nothing to protect itself at the very point whence our former misfortunes came, and where also to-day is to be found one of our most subtle, and yet one of the most dangerous, forms of peril that has ever threatened any republican form of government. How astounding, that there should be so much puerile legislation as to leave no time for that which is most vital!

It is as clear as a November sky, also, that delay in correct educational measures invites peril from a still more specific quarter, to which allusion was made in the introduction of this address. A moment's reflection is ample to show that our next-door neighbors are, on political grounds, not the most desirable. No one can say that Spanish and Cuban troubles will not result in dividing those islands into different States, nor that those States will not ask to be admitted into the Union; if the request is made, who doubts that they will be received, and thenceforth be represented in our Congress. Such results need not alarm us; let those States be welcomed? But, some one replies, These will be Roman Catholic States. True, yet we think God will control them; if so, we shall not be Romanized, but they will be Protestantized.

But, again: there is no reasonable doubt that the outbreak along the Mexican borders will continue. The Romish priests do not care to have peace; with such sentiments on their part, there can be no peace. We have grounds for supposing that they provoke hostilities and smile at depredations. There will be successful efforts, anon, to divide Mexico into several States; this done, they will ask to be received into the Union; their request will be granted, and they, too, will be represented in Congress. And still there may be no occasion for alarm; let these Mexican States receive a hearty welcome. But, it is replied, These also will be Roman Catholic States. True, yet God can control them; if so, their allegiance to the Pope will eventuate in loyalty to the State.

Still again: we have reason for the statement that the leading Roman Catholics of the Canadas are ready to provoke any form of disturbance which would be likely to result in their accession to the United States. The possible methods are so numerous that it is, at the present moment, difficult to say which is the more probable. But the final outcome, if we are not mistaken, favored, as it will be, by the Catholic world, is inevitable. More States enter the Union, and are represented in Congress, and, notwithstanding it may seem perilous, we hesitate not to say, let these Northern territories also be added. But, some one replies, these too will be Roman Catholic States. True, yet God will probably control them; and if he does, the leaven of republicanism and of Protestantism will leaven the whole continent. That these surrounding neighbors are Romanists is hardly the fault of the Republic. That we admit them to the blessings of the best government on earth, can hardly be a sin. Hence, we may confidently look for divine intervention; if this is granted, all is safe.

But once more, as to the freedmen. God has seen their wrongs. He sees that the Government, which owes them almost more than it can ever pay, nevertheless refuses the aid and emancipation from ignorance which he has commanded.

He is allowing the nation to pave its way to an inevitable overthrow. Because the Government will not discharge its obligations to the colored people, God may allow the Roman Catholic Church, which for ten centuries has been the most pronounced, unscrupulous, and relentless enemy of all free institutions, to take to itself five millions of our citizens. He is allowing the Southern Democrat to sell himself and his ex-slave to Romanism, while Romanism pledges itself to drop the secession Democratic ballot, even though it wrecks the Republic; this is Rome's pleasure. Have we not yet learned that this foe of liberty "never surrenders? That she temporizes, but always renews the battle at the fitting moment? That, if defeated in one country, she renews the conflict in another? That she has not failed to see her danger in Europe and her hope in America? That her plans here are deeply laid and quietly but zealously pursued? That in no part of the nation is this more marked than among the freedmen of the South? That her success with them is more apparent every day. Protestants may not realize it till the danger is imminent. But, whether realized sooner or later, Americans have here one of the conflicts of this new century.

Prussia is wise; she sees the danger, and with surprising boldness defies the enemy. But America is blindfolded, and bows in weak submission. Gladstone sees the impending struggle in England, and utters his courageous and prophetic warnings. But the Republic has no Gladstone, and Congress is dumb as a corpse. But, does some one say? God can control. True, God *can* control. He can work miracles; he can do wonders. Nevertheless, if the Congress of the United States continues recreant, God will *not* control, and he will not delay, but will lash this nation with the rod of his wrath. Unless there is a change of policy, the Romanist, in the form of a black man, shall be the ordained instrument of infliction. It sometimes seems that the bit of paper dropped from black and brawny fingers is to seal, one way or the other, our national destiny. How much like a providence of God it would be, if those black men, in some impending crisis, should be left to wreck the Republic which has so brutally wronged them.

One of the wisest of our bishops has spoken words which deserve a place in all our councils: "The black, blind giant that we have admitted to the temple of Liberty, if only his eyes be couched, may buttress its walls; but if left blind, he may, in some political crisis, where the beams are in equipoise, pull the fair fabric to the ground."

Why will not our Congress listen? Are its eyes blinded past recovery, and its ears fatally and forever deafened? If it will educate and christianize these colored populations, or if it will aid us in accomplishing the work, our country is safe, and will shortly have ampler protection than all her navies and armies combined can afford. We venture the assertion that the conduct of the Government within the next five years, or perhaps during the present session of Congress, will be decisive as to our national existence. Unless something is done other than has been done, those who stand where we do, a century hence, will wonder that we were so blind as not to displace our sentimental bunting at this first centennial, and wreathe our republican standard with the mourner's crape; or they will ask why we did not invite the nations to a funeral, rather than to the exhibition of our proud celebrations. But, the politician replies, We can do nothing. This work does not come within the province of the general Government. There is no way we can assist your societies, nor any way we can educate the freedmen. These are State matters. State matters! The Government do nothing! O, America, you can not do *nothing* much longer. But, the politician continues, There is no way in which we can do more. No way! No way! Then, O God, smite the narrow politician, and give us a statesman, who has wit and courage enough, when there is no way, to *make* one, and thus save the nation from the wrath and indignation of a justly provoked heaven.

But, lastly: If constantly vanishing opportunities and Divine Providence afford ground for a plea to the Church and to the National Government, much more do they furnish occasion for us *to plead directly with the Southern States.* At the close of the war was their golden age. Then was the time to have returned to peaceful industries and virtuous living. Had this been done, who can paint the prosperity which would have crowned that land which is to-day bankrupt and disconsolate? The opportunity came; Northern capitalists looked southward, but, after being insulted and robbed, returned, leaving behind them, for the most part, adventurers, who, availing themselves of the colored vote, gained personal advantages, to the detriment of the State interests; for this condition the Southern people have none to blame but themselves. Then, too, was the time to have made the freedmen more profitable to the planter than ever the bondman had been. These colored races have an instinctive fidelity to law and order, and could have been easily controlled. They felt no revenge for past wrongs; they did not murder their old masters, nor fire their cities, nor desolate their lands. It would not have surprised us at the North, had these people run into all possible excesses after their emancipation; and yet, notwithstanding the fears and prophecies of many to the contrary, these millions entered upon their new life quietly, as if they desired to show themselves qualified and in every way worthy of their new trusts. They were not exorbitant in their demands. They had been schooled not to expect much in this world; their hopes and aspirations had been centered upon the hereafter; it was beyond Jordan that they hoped to have their wrongs righted. Yes, easily, very easily could they have been controlled, and then elevated. But the treatment they have received has somewhat hardened them. Distressed and discouraged, the colored man yesterday was sullen. To-day he is laying aside the Primer and Bible. To-morrow the tempest will darken the sky, the earthquake will yawn in its madness, and the hands of the black man may nervously clutch at the knife and the fire-brand.

"God comes with leaden feet," says the proverb, "but strikes with an iron fist." The law of gravitation is a law of justice; there can be no question upon what part of the country the avenging blows will smite heaviest. Our earnest hopes for the better recall the eloquent words of Mr. Lincoln's last inaugural: "Fondly do we hope, fervently do we pray, that this mighty scourge of war may speedily pass away. Yet if God wills that it continue until all the wealth piled by the bondman's two hundred and fifty years of unrequited toil shall be sunk, and until every drop of blood drawn with the lash shall be paid by another drawn with the sword, as was said three thousand years ago, so still it must be said, "'the judgments of the Lord are true and righteous altogether.'" But it must be admitted, even by the Southerner, that our Freedmen's Aid Society has taxed itself to avert the evils of such a day. It has tried to do this in the only effectual way possible; namely, by making of colored people intelligent and Christian citizens. What a sublime opportunity there has been for the Church, North and South, to unite in this philanthropic and Christ-like service!

When the war closed, Northern Christians, feeling their obligations to the colored race, and seeing, in part, the magnificent missionary possibilities already mentioned, went immediately to the relief of that people. Not that they did not love their Northern homes and superior privileges better; not that they would do any wrong to any Southerner; not that they would be intruders upon Southern soil; but they heartily proffered this service because they loved him for whom Christ died. They saw that many of the colored people had minds capable of the highest culture, and that the souls of all were precious, and that multitudes had been washed white in the blood of the Redeemer. The Northern missionary desired to place, in the hands of those who had been denied educational privileges, the Primer, that they might learn to read the Bible. We repeat, they did this, not because of hatred, either to the task-master, or to the secessionist, or to the rebel soldier, but because God commanded them to discharge this duty.

We saw a traveler, just delivered from the house of bondage, but struck down on the threshold and left wounded by the road-side. We dared not pass him by. We had been taught in our Northern homes, that we must bind up these wounds, that we must take that man to some wayside inn until he be somewhat recovered. As Christians we could not have done otherwise; and yet, in rendering this Christian work, what reception did we meet at the hands of those called Christians? We entered that country—*our* country—for a Christ-like purpose, and have remained there, not only treated as no Christian should be, but at the peril of our lives. We almost hope the world will not believe the statement, but in those Southern States is found the only place, in any civilized, or half-civilized land on earth, where the American citizen is neither protected nor respected, and where the self-sacrificing minister of Christ is insecure day and night while prosecuting his Christian work. How long, O Lord, how long? What but a fearful tempest can clear that Southern atmosphere?*

There are noble Christian women who have left delightful homes in the North, where every comfort was enjoyed, for the sole purpose of bringing these poor blacks to Christ. They have been obliged to sell their furniture, in some instances, to buy food, yet they have not faltered. "I do not ask for a salary," writes one of these lady teachers, "only enough to sustain me while I toil for these poor people for whom Christ died?" Such has been their devotion; and yet I blush to speak of the treatment they have received at your hands, Southern Christian women. You have not spoken to those self-sacrificing and devoted teachers; nay, you have scorned them when passing the street; you have not visited them when sick, nor given them a cup of cold water when thirst-stricken. I risk not the possibility of contradiction when saying, that treatment like this has not been witnessed on earth since earth witnessed the advent of Christianity. †

---

* The following may be taken as representative accounts coming from those now engaged in the Southern work. A teacher in ―――― writes thus:

"Sometimes we get to thinking that times are better than they have been; then accounts of new outrages come to us, showing us how uncertain is our security, except as we feel secure in God's hands. We have no human protection. Last Saturday we received a letter from a neighboring presiding elder, stating that there had just been an attempt to assassinate him, and he had been obliged to leave the place, where he was helping to carry on a meeting."

"Bands of armed and masked men are prowling around nights, whipping some and murdering others. Politicians, at a public meeting, have threatened our schools, and, being isolated from every human protection, we are in great fear and peril. I have devoted the nights to watching, for the protection of life, and to guarding our buildings against fire. To be for weeks in constant expectation of being murdered or burned out, and without losing faith in God, is something of a strain on the nerves. Mr. ―――― who assisted me last year, and two other white teachers who were teaching a short distance west of us, were allowed twenty-four hours to leave."

† From a Northern minister, now in the South, we have the following: "We are shut out from all white society, until it is really a treat to have a white child speak to us. My wife has spoken but to two white women since we came here, and then only on business." We could indefinitely multiply this class of correspondence.

Can there be reasonable expectation that the people of God will be required to suffer this abuse without end? or that such rare opportunities for the South to unite with the North in restoring peace and christianizing the freedmen will be continued? Such continuance would contradict the universal methods of God's providence.*

But more than this. There are wrongs of a darker shade; those which have been continued to that wounded man, stripped and left half dead, whose flowing wounds we have been trying to stanch. That story is so fearful and long that we can not commence it. But God is the witness that blow after blow is even now inflicted upon them; blows entirely unprovoked.†

---

* We read, with much interest, lately, the following from one of our teachers in Georgia: "My impression is that the South will be devastated by another war. Leading men here assert that the United States Government must pay for the slaves it emancipated. The bad passions which made the former war are as prevalent, as unreasonable, as furious, as they were fifteen years ago. I would not wonder if we were fleeing from Georgia for our lives in less than a year; and, as I review history, past and present, of ours and other lands, I fear that God will make this whole land a wilderness. The work has begun. The lands are impoverished; the people are sowing dragon's teeth; and the fate of Babylon and Nineveh awaits us! Centuries of wrong and oppression and suffering cry unto God for vengeance. May God have mercy upon us, when he draws his sword and bends his bow."

† One of our colored preachers writes thus: "The White Leagues are unfavorable to our education and enlightenment, and we tremble for future developments. I have lived in this country for the past forty-five years, but never before have I witnessed such dreadfully discouraging prospects."

One of our teachers in —— writes thus: "Every means is being taken to frighten and intimidate the colored people, with the hope of being able to keep them away from the elections. Great efforts are being made by the Southern whites to keep the freedmen out of school, such as warning them that their lives will not be safe if they go, and refusing to pay them money for their labor. Mr. ——, a young man twenty-one years of age, came here from his home, a distance of twenty miles, most of the way in the night, avoiding main roads, taking unfrequented paths through the woods, to avoid attracting attention. Every colored man seen moving round through the country must give an account of himself and his business. Mr. —— does not dare return to his home during term-time. One of the young men who attended school here last Winter has been working all Summer and Fall for a white man, and saving every thing to help him get an education. When his wages amounted to upward of a hundred dollars, he decided to go to school, asked for his money, and was refused, with the assertion, from his employer, that 'none of his money

When we reflect that God is training this people to do a missionary work of the greatest magnitude, we tremble for those who dare thus afflict them. The speaker before one of the Southern colleges, at a late commencement, must have thought otherwise, and must have imagined that the universe is really orphaned, when saying that the negro is in the way, significantly asking, "Why cumbereth he the ground?"

Why cumbereth he the ground! Is that the Southern man's inquiry? The impertinent question deserves but one answer: *The colored man has earned his right to that soil, and God is not dead.* If we mistake not, he designs that the black man shall yet have a peaceful home in those Southern States; woe to those who attempt to prevent it. If there is no other way to secure this result, Jehovah may allow continued aggravations to exasperate the freedmen; and then he may say to them, as he did to the children of Israel, "Ye shall drive out all the inhabitants of the land from before you." *

We have to make the confession that it greatly troubles us to know how God can avert these implied calamities. He is an especial friend of the poor and the oppressed. He hears every prayer; he counts every sigh. He has said: "For the oppression of the poor, for the sighing of the needy, will I arise;" "for the Lord will plead their cause, and spoil the soul of those that spoil them." He can not delay much longer. Those colored children are beginning to lose faith in God. He has pledged himself to hear their prayers; they are beginning to disbelieve in prayer. His kingdom, seemingly, is imperiled if he delays. Must not God avenge those who cry day and night unto him, though he bear long with them? "I tell you," is our Lord's assurance, "that he will avenge them speedily."

If that significant and menacing question, "Why cumbereth he the ground?" expresses the prevailing sentiment South— when the question was asked, it was vociferously cheered--

---

should go to send a nigger to school.' As there is no redress here for the poor colored man, he could only go to work again for his bread. This is only one of hundreds of such cases."

Of the slaughter of thousands of these innocent colored people we do not speak. A picture is suggested which we dare not sketch.

* Numbers xxxiii, 50-56.

and if these sorrowing children continue to have multiplied wrongs heaped upon them, the Almighty, in pure self-defense, may be forced to say to these outraged people: "Thou art my battle-ax and weapons of war; for with thee will I break in pieces, . . . and with thee will I destroy. . . . With thee will I break in pieces men and women; and with thee will I break in pieces old and young, and with thee will I break in pieces the young man and the maid; I will also break in pieces with thee the shepherd and his flock; and with thee will I break in pieces the husbandman and his yoke of oxen, and with thee will I break in pieces captains and rulers." "Art thou not from everlasting, O Lord, my God? . . . O Lord, thou hast ordained them for judgment, . . . and thou hast established them for correction."*

O, ye Southern white men, blood of our blood, withhold! Do not strike another blow. You are vainly attempting to thwart the onward and majestic movements of God's providences. You are killing God's missionaries, and are binding Christ again to the cross; these crimes, if continued, will admit of no expiation.

It may be false, but there is a vision of fearful possibilities rising before us, whose banishment we have sought, but it remains:

    Is seen a black and calloused hand;
    It seizes quick and flings abroad
      A fire-brand.

Lurid skies appear; at morn, at eve the same;
Roofs of city and of village are aflame;
Gleaming brands and gleaming eyes terrific glare;
Ashes in the sunny South are every-where.

    Is seen a hand of darker shade;
    It seizes quick and wields in might
      A crimson blade.

Women mad with dread, and with disheveled hair,
Screech murder! the bloody hand does not forbear;
Deeply craped and crimsoned now is all that's fair;
Hush!, the mangled corse is lying every-where.

Over the sunny land descends a lengthened night;
Tempest, cloud, and darkness thickly shroud the light.
  . . . .

---

* Jer. li, 20-23; Hab. i, 12.

Nights must have an end. The sun at length does rise;
Other scenes and visions gayly greet mine eyes,
Gleeful children, homes and lands enchanting fair.
Freedmen are enlightened, honored freemen there;
'T is now another race; forgotten are the dead;
Blessed is the sunny South; but fifty years are fled.

To avert these possibilities that lie in the path of the redemption of our land, O, Church of God, O, nation of the free, O, ye men of the South, unite to protect and aid these poor people, who have so long borne our oppressions.

Rev. Dr. Walden, of Cincinnati, was introduced, and delivered an able address, of which the following is the substance:

At this late hour my remarks must be brief, and shall be confined to some of the results of personal observation. One reason for the invitation which brings me before you is the fact of my having been officially connected with the early movements in the West in behalf of the freedmen. The report and the address to which you have listened are so comprehensive that what I may say shall indicate my interest in the cause, rather than add to the interest of this meeting.

Our Methodist people must every-where come to regard the work of our Freedmen's Aid Society as providential—to view it in the light, in which, all along, it has been seen by those who have studied its relations, and felt the force of its demands. That it is a work ordained of Heaven, with claims upon every Christian, is amply illustrated by facts which are now historic. It has its place in plans devised by a prescience, and developed by a power, that were divine. Had emancipation been the object—not the incident—of the great war, provision to meet the necessities of the emancipated would have been an obvious duty; but our nation learned the lesson of freedom only through the severe discipline of successive disasters, and so slowly, too, that for months, multitudes, made homeless by the stroke that made them free, had no public care. But they were not uncared for; He who, despite the traditions of the nation, appointed their deliverance, had by his Spirit moved upon the hearts of those who were to be their friends. Soon after escaping slaves were declared "contraband of war"—a significant event now almost crowded out of view—a work of relief was begun in their behalf and well organized before freedom was proclaimed.

This work appealed to the sympathies of the people—sympathies daily quickened by the painful incidents of the war; it was a movement in behalf of real sufferers—of those who suffered because of a struggle in the results of which it did not yet appear they had any interest. Through generations the people of the North had seemed insensible to their miseries as slaves; but now the appeal came when every humane feeling was aroused by scenes of the field and hospital. It was God's time; and the unwonted interest in the despised race was such that private charities supplied the service for which the Government was not prepared.

Education speedily followed physical relief, and for years the two went hand in hand. What awakened mind that had slumbered for generations? What quickened into being the universal passion to read and write? What made the hand seize, with a miser's nervous grasp, the book and the pen? The events of the war? The fact of emancipation? These are not effect and cause. What moved Christian men and women—mark you, Christian, not infidel, men and women—in places widely removed from each other, to become teachers among the "contrabands" before they were known as freedmen? He, and He only, who, with power to achieve, had undertaken in their behalf. So, when freedom became a fact, through the President's proclamation, there were organizations already in the field to meet the emancipated with the means both of relief and education.

In this undenominational work, so marked in its rise and history, the Freedmen's Aid Society of the Methodist Episcopal Church had its origin;—not the result of a plan projected by our Church, but a direct growth from a charity that commanded the sympathies of all Christian people;—the natural offshoot of a vine of blessing planted by the divine hand. It took form in a conviction, shared by every leading Christian denomination, that among the freedmen was opened the most promising mission-field before the Church. When the sister and co-operative denominations had each moved off on the line of a denominational work, our Society was organized, without ecclesiastical authority, by a few who had studied the field from the first; once organized, it was seen to be right, and the Church received it as its own.

The basal idea of this Society was, that missions among the freedmen could not be successful—could not give to the Church they should plant the conditions of strength and perpetuity—so far as these depend upon human agencies—without employing the school as one of the means. Because of that desire to learn which had the fervency of a passion, the missionary, whose Church sent the teacher as well, had an open door to his people. Again, it brought to his aid, in the Sunday-school and elsewhere, those who could be most helpful. Providence has never opened a field to which nobler laborers than these teachers have gone. Long before a missionary had been sent to the freedmen, Christian men and women had become their teachers; before this Society had a being, it was my privilege—I count it an honor—to commission and send to the South four hundred teachers—Christians of sterling worth; among them accomplished young women, from homes possessed of every thing that heart could wish, who, constrained by the love of Christ, hastened to the self-sought task of teaching the young and the old, and, when not in school, distributing the means of relief to the needy and suffering; and this, too, where, far from home, they were ostracized by their Southern white sisters for this service to Christ's poor. This educational work has given to our missionaries a corps of helpers such as these.

That people are to be evangelized and elevated, and it must be chiefly by their own efforts, directed and encouraged, in the beginning, by those upon whose hearts the duty is laid. Their teachers and preachers must come up among themselves. It is no reflection—only the statement of a law—to say that preachers and teachers of their own number can be more helpful to them, can best reach their conditions. Again, every one who rises into an intelligent leader among them, either as preacher or teacher, illustrates what others may do, and thereby becomes an inspiration to noble purposes and manly endeavor. And further, our Church, planted among them, welcomed by them, is to stand and prosper; but, in order to this, there must be a membership from which intelligent men and women may be taken for our leaders, stewards, and other office-bearers.

By this Society we are connected with public questions—not questions of party, but of State—that commend it to the Christian patriot. The colored man is a voter—a citizen with its highest prerogative—and this means a power for good or for evil in society. The moral condition of our country is affected by the character of those who hold the ballot. It is not the presence of frugal foreign laborers and tradesmen and their households, but of foreign voters, that has trenched upon the observance of the American Sabbath, modified laws that guaranteed this element of religious toleration and effected other conservative laws, and carried many of the lax moral notions into government.

But as voters, the colored men have greater power than these. They are more numerous; in 1870, of the 2,914,736 voters in the former Slave States, 931,665 were colored men—nearly one-third of the entire voting population. Again, they are more localized; they are so distributed that they have the majority in South Carolina and Mississippi, and can hold the balance of power in several other States. The concentration of certain classes of voters makes self-government in some of our cities a mockery; so this concentration of the freedmen in one section augments their power for weal or woe to the State.

It is the interest of religion that our free Government shall stand—and that it become more pure and perfect—but its perpetuity and purity must result largely from the intelligence of the voters. *The only safe condition of universal suffrage is universal education.* The one we have—the other must be reached. Without any connection with the Government, the Church may plan to help forward a work which conserves the public good. Her schools are not planted to educate voters, but her Freedmen's Aid Society, and other kindred societies, have demonstrated, what was long and sturdily denied, that the colored people have capacity to learn; and, while every teacher she commissions goes in the direct interest of religion, each one helps to create a sentiment that will, sooner or later, demand the American free-school system.

In this connection I will say that universal education being the means of national security, our Church, both ministers and people, should move solidly in its favor. If this can only be secured by compulsory measures, then I say, as I have often said before, let such be adopted. We are coming, as a people, to favor this. During the past ten years, in the line of official duties, I have attended nearly every Annual Conference in the West and South, and in addresses before them have expressed my firm conviction, formed years ago when more directly connected with this educational work, that *the State has an interest in the child—the future man or woman—in view of which, it should demand, for every one, a common education in public or private schools;* and the sentiment has often been received with approval. I believe that our people favor a free-school system that shall be universal, and, to that end, if need be, compulsory. The schools of our Society are preparing the way for such a system in the South.

Further, if the general Government adopts, at large cost, measures of defense, why should not education have its care and support? If subsidies can be given to railroads to develop the resources of the country, why may not appropriations be made and measures adopted to foster intelligence? If large grants could be made to the States to encourage so-called Agricultural Colleges, why may not grants be made to the Southern States, impoverished as they are, to establish common-schools—the colleges of the people? Let this be done by Congress during the next year, and it will be the noblest monument that will commemorate our nation's first Centennial.

In speaking of our missions among the freedmen, I should have said that they differ from all others in our country, in that, like our foreign work, they need the school. In the newest States, the pioneer preacher finds the school planted with the settlement. Where there is mission work in the older conferences, schools exist by the support of the State. Only those who labor among the freedmen are without these potent agencies, and for them the Missionary Society has no provision. But for the Freedmen's Aid Society, the work in this inviting and prosperous field would move slowly on, without the inspiration that it now receives from helpful and devoted teachers, and the re-enforcements that come from the halls of thrifty normal schools and rising colleges.

In this work we can not await the slow processes of the past; if we did, the freedman could not abide our time. He comes upon the stage—a man—at an important juncture in human affairs—in a period of tireless activity; at a time when art and science give the skilled and cultured an imperial dominion over nature; when the world moves as never before, and peoples rise instinct with a new life; and here and now, under these conditions, he must hold his way! But more—he begins his struggle beside the Caucasian, the proud race that has led in the march of the world for centuries. He takes his place beside the Anglo-Saxon, the most active and indomitable branch of this race. He comes to the ballot—the seal of equality and sovereignity—at a time when statesmen are few, and swarming politicians, most sordid and unscrupulous, to compass their own ends, will take advantage of his ignorance, and control his franchise to his own hurt. He comes before the Church when the forces opposed to a holy, spiritual, and experimental religion, are most persistent and wily in their craft, and the influences are most active that would turn him from the simple and saving faith of the Gospel.

The position of this people is a crucial one, and one that should enlist in their behalf our warmest sympathies and our helpfulness. Their best security is religion and education; these must go to them hand in hand; our missionaries must carry to them the Gospel, and our Freedmen's Aid Society must be supported in maintaining and multiplying its schools until the several States, earnestly and in good faith, place their hand to the work, or until the nation puts in force a system that shall be national and American.

Every Christian Church has a duty here, but God has honored Methodism by putting upon her the heaviest obligation. This is seen in that he has favored our Church with material prosperity as well as spiritual. During the last ten years, her membership has increased seventy per cent, while the aggregate value of her churches and parsonages has increased one hundred and sixty per cent. This means a membership of growing wealth. During the same decade, the number of her churches has increased fifty-five per cent—their aggregate value nearly one hundred and thirty per cent; the number of her parsonages sixty per cent—their aggregate value more than one hundred and twenty per cent. These infallible signs of material prosperity mean that God has intrusted her membership with large resources to meet large responsibilities,—appointed them stewards of the wealth from which her work among the freedmen, which is His work, should have an abundant support.

Again, this is seen in that He has given our Church positions of strength among the freedmen. From the Annual Report you have learned the number, power, and location of our schools. Remember that our Church was the last to turn from the undenominational work—hence the last to enter the field for a special service—and then, running your eye from the Delaware to the Rio Grande, study in their relation to the South, the commercial and social centers, where the schools of this, her Society, are firmly established.

Again, our Church has had a welcome such as no other, whose base is in the North, has received. One of the most active, with an antislavery record, with large contributions for its work, with abundant aid from Government, with good buildings and devoted teachers, has fewer churches than schools, fewer Church-members than pupils; while our Church, within ten years, has enrolled in her ranks nearly two hundred thousand freedmen, and every-where they have hailed her coming with delight—"Welcome, welcome, to the Old John Wesley Church."

Finally, this obligation is seen in the call of Methodism to evangelize the lowly masses. To these she has carried the Gospel; among these her foundations have been laid; from these she has recruited her membership; and now, with teachers at her command, with evangelists waiting her summons, with wealth intrusted to her people, she is called to work for the salvation of the freedmen—of the poor and the lowly in masses such as she never reached before—in fields where the harvest is ripest for her reapers.

www.ingramcontent.com/pod-product-compliance
Lightning Source LLC
Chambersburg PA
CBHW032238080426
42735CB00008B/910